*What Jesus Saw
from the Cross*

2/20/15

Dear Jackie

I thought you might enjoy this book on our Lenten journey..

God Bless you always!

W/Love & Friendship

A. G. Sertillanges

What Jesus Saw
from the Cross

SOPHIA INSTITUTE PRESS
Manchester, New Hampshire

What Jesus Saw from the Cross was published in French as *Ce que Jésus voyait du haut de la croix* by Ernest Flammarion of Paris in 1930. An English translation was published originally by Clonmore & Reynolds Ltd. in Dublin in 1948. This 1996 edition is based on the 1948 translation but has been edited to conform it to standard modern English usage and to correct other infelicities in the text. Explanatory footnotes have been added throughout.

On the cover: *Crucifixion* (Jerusalem with temple and turreted walls), contemporary copy of a lost painting by van Eyck (c. 1530) / Museum of Fine Arts, Budapest, Hungary / Lessing Photo Archive.
Circular detail: *Crucifixion* (oil on panel), Brea, Ludovico (c.1450-1523) / Church of Cimiez, Nice, France / Giraudon / The Bridgeman Art Library International.

Sophia Institute Press
Box 5284, Manchester, NH 03108
1-800-888-9344
www.sophiainstitute.com
Sophia Institute Press® is a registered trademark of Sophia Institute.

Nihil obstat: Ernest Messenger, *Censor deputatus*
Imprimatur: Joseph Butt, *Vicar General, Westmonasterii*, January 8, 1937

Library of Congress Cataloging-in-Publication Data

Sertillanges, A. G. (Antonin Gilbert), 1863-1948.
  [Ce que Jésus voyait du haut de la croix. English]
  What Jesus saw from the cross / A. G. Sertillanges
      p. cm.
  Originally published: Dublin : Clonmore & Reynolds Ltd., 1948.
  Includes bibliographical references.
  ISBN 0-918477-25-5 (hdbk.)—ISBN 0-918477-37-9 (pbk.)
  1. Jesus Christ—Crucifixion. I. Title.

BT450.S4213 1996
232.96'3—dc20   94-42378 CIP

Contents

What Jesus Saw
from the Cross

_____

Editor's Note: The biblical references in these pages are based on the Douay-Rheims edition of the Old and New Testaments. Where appropriate, quotations from the Psalms and some of the historical books of the Bible have been cross-referenced with the differing names and enumeration in the Revised Standard Version using the following symbol: (RSV=).

Prologue

St. Paul exhorts us to "put on Jesus Christ,"[1] and his words, understood in the spiritual sense in which he intended them, are of immeasurable importance. However, there is perhaps another sense in which it is not impossible, nor without importance, to put on Jesus Christ.

We may put on Jesus Christ in imagination, placing ourselves not at the foot of the Cross, nor before it, but upon it, with head bowed beneath the inscription, wearing the crown of thorns, pierced by the nails, feeling the cold, rough wood between our shoulders. In short, we can make our own the sphere of vision and the emotions that were His, seeing with His eyes and feeling with His heart, remembering, judging, and foreseeing with Him so that, still in this same sense of imagining that we have changed places with Him, it is no longer we who live but Christ who lives in us.[2]

[1] Rom. 13:14.
[2] Gal. 2:20.

3

It was in Jerusalem that this thought came to me, while I stood (as I frequently did) on a spot which is uniquely suggestive of such reflections.

On the terrace of the Greeks overlooking the atrium of the Holy Sepulcher, a few paces from the great dome, is a small stone cupola surmounted by a cross. It can be reached quite easily, and you may stand there and linger. If you now face Jerusalem, which is spread before your eyes, making allowances for the changes operated by time, you are confronted with the same panorama as met the gaze of the divine Master.

According to the most careful calculations and on the authority of one who knows the archaeology of the Holy Land better than anyone of the present day,[3] the iron cross which you are touching there marks, within a few inches, the level and the place once occupied by the divine countenance. A striking thought, which recalls the words of St. Cyril of Jerusalem as he preached at the Holy Sepulcher: "How many others are able only to hear, while we can see and touch!"

The scene of the crucifixion is today changed beyond recognition; the mere mention of my observation post would be sufficient to show this. But it is possible to reconstruct it without any great difficulty. A few doubtful points remain to be settled, and torturing those doubts are — for it is not easy to reconcile ourselves to the regrettable fact that we cannot at this moment with certainty trace out the Way of the Cross. But the remainder of the sacred site is happily known to us. Its general lines are indicated for us by the hills that encircle Golgotha. The knolls, the valleys, partly

---

[3] Père H. Vincent, author of the archaeological, and to some extent also of the historical part of the great work *Jérusalem: Recherches de topographie, d'archéologie et d'histoire* by H. Vincent and F. M. Abel (Paris: Garabalda, 1912-1926).

filled but plainly discernible, still remain; the roads are determined by the formation of the ground and by immutable directions. The ruins visible here and there, the excavations made in recent times, the comparative study of texts and of facts enable us to recognize and even to establish with precision the theater of the drama. We may feel the thrill of reality.

Let us, then, without further delay open our eyes, the eyes of our body and the eyes of our intelligence, with Jesus Christ. As we "put on" Jesus Christ let us wed ourselves to His mind and His heart. So it may be that the invisible world in which His soul moves will appear more vividly to us, and perhaps we may be granted the grace of a more intimate union with Him.

A. G. Sertillanges
Jerusalem
Holy Thursday Evening

1

The View from the Cross

When Jesus leaves the praetorium,[4] it is about twelve o'clock, in Jerusalem the sultriest hour of the day.

It is springtime — March 20th at the earliest, April 17th at the latest — but spring in the Holy Land has none of the charm of our April. Spring is the season of uncertain weather; one day will be beautiful, the next may bring snow or stifling heat. It is the season of the Khamsin, the hot, depressing wind that comes from the southwest.

Jesus is carrying His Cross. To His neck, probably, is attached the placard two feet square, whitened with chalk, which will be nailed to the Cross to advertise the nature of His crime. He is preceded by a mounted centurion and escorted by a band of soldiers. For company Jesus has two thieves whom they have decided to execute with Him. In front, behind, and around Him is an inquisitive or hostile mob.

---

[4] The state residence of a Roman official from which he exercises his political and juridical authority.

For some two hundred yards in a direct line, but rather more through the network of narrow streets, their way lies downhill through the town. Then the road slopes upwards, always winding, bringing the total distance to five hundred yards. The procession thus reaches the Gate of Ephraim, otherwise called the Gate of the Square because it opens upon a square esplanade, bounded by a right-angled corner in the walls. This was later to become the Roman forum.

The Gate of Ephraim is a *redan* gate. That is, it forms a salient angle [pointing outward instead of inward], so that the entrance is from north to south and the exit from east to west. It is interesting to recall that in a Greek convent nearby, an ancient step is preserved upon which Jesus may have trod as He carried His Cross.

Immediately after He crossed the threshold, Jesus stood face-to-face with His tomb.

There was nothing gloomy about the prospect, in spite of the tombs, which were a common feature of the wealthy properties of the period. The gate between that of Ephraim and that of Jaffa was called the Gate of Gardens; and in fact all the slopes of Gareb, the hill opposite, were under cultivation.

Olives formed the chief part of the vegetation, but there were also citrons, figs, nuts, and pomegranates. Many birds made their nests in the branches of these trees, swallows and martins making merry in the springtime, along with sparrows, lapwings, cuckoos, thrushes, and turtledoves. Nor was there any lack of flowers. The place was carpeted with cyclamens, the flower of rocky ground, wild daffodils, irises, fennel, poppies, and daisies, and especially the red anemone. Perhaps, too, there was the lily of the field that vies with the glory of Solomon[5] — a flower which glitters like a

---

[5] Luke 12:27.

stained-glass window when the sun shines upon it, but in the shade has the dull hue of dried blood.

There, too, were the famous flowers of Calvary: those tiny blossoms that never seem to die, sprouting today in the same places as yesterday. Jesus, who loved them, mingled His blood with their crimson drops; and the robin redbreast of legend, the meditative dove of the Psalm,[6] and perhaps the owl, too, attracted by the great darkness, were there to soothe Him in death.

Once on a Good Friday about three o'clock in the afternoon, I was in my favorite spot — on the terrace which I mentioned above — when I saw the air suddenly filled with a cloud of swallows flying thickly together and filling the surrounding space with their cries. The little iron cross which now stands in the place of the great gibbet was caught in the network of their lines of flight; to and fro the shrill and fleeting cries crossed and recrossed one another. It was a festival, and it was a reminder of death. Who knows but that Jesus in the depths of His agony heard and welcomed with a sad smile another such exquisite canticle.

We have spoken of Calvary, and we have not yet located this "mountain" which occupies so important a place in our thoughts. It is difficult enough to locate it by our account, and the pilgrim on the spot, unless forewarned, would find it still more difficult to place it near the medieval *parvis* that leads to it.[7]

The fact is that Calvary is not a mountain at all; it is not even a hill, unless you would dignify by that name what is little more

---

[6] Ps. 67:14 (RSV = Ps. 68:13).

[7] A *parvis* is an enclosed area or court in front of a building, especially a cathedral or church.

than a knoll in a field. If the esplanade of sixty yards in front of the Gate of Ephraim had not yet been levelled — and had it been, in point of fact? — the ascent to Calvary would have been almost imperceptible. This chalky mound stood not more than sixteen feet above the roads which wound around its base; it rose rather abruptly from the western side, but quite gradually from the east and southeast, the way by which Jesus approached it.

However, our Lord's observation post dominates the town. When the gibbet has been erected, its highest point will be another ten feet above the level of the ground, and the gaze of the Crucified may range over the whole horizon.

In front of Him Jesus will see the Gate of Ephraim at a distance of eighty yards, the Temple at a quarter of a mile, the tower of Antonia at four hundred yards, and at seven hundred yards the great southeastern corner, or the "pinnacle" from which Satan had wanted Him to cast Himself down.[8]

Then He will see the surrounding country. North-northeast, almost due north, are the slopes of Nabi-Samouël, the "high place" of Gibeon where Solomon had his dream of wisdom[9] and where the unhappy Rizpah protected her sons against the vultures.[10] Then He will see Mizpah, where the faithful Maccabees worshipped while awaiting their entry into Jerusalem.[11]

To the northeast exactly is Mount Scopus, where Alexander[12] once quailed before the majesty of the high priest; where Cestius

---

[8] Matt. 4:5-6; Luke 4:9-10.

[9] 3 Kings 3:4-5 (RSV = 1 Kings 3:4-5).

[10] 2 Kings 21:10 (RSV = 2 Sam. 21:10).

[11] 1 Macc. 3:46.

[12] Alexander (356-323 B.C.), commonly known as "the Great," was the Macedonian king who conquered large portions of the Mediterranean basin, including the Holy Land, and who established Greek culture throughout the territory he conquered.

Gallus and Titus[13] encamped when the days of Israel were accomplished; where later the soldiers of Godfrey de Bouillon made their advance[14] — a solemn approach to the city, which since the days of Nebuchadnezzar,[15] Sennacherib, and Tiglath-pileser[16] has always been an object of delight or of desire.

To the east is the Mount of Olives, which holds a predominant place in the life of Jesus as a consequence of the memories evoked by its lower reaches, its slopes, its summit, its surroundings, its villages, and its roads. And therefore we shall dwell upon it in these pages.

To the right of the Mount of Olives, across the brook Kedron, is a strip of burnt and arid desert, behind which you can smell the Dead Sea and see the unbroken line of the mountains of Moab, with the fringe of mist at their base which rises from those heavy waters. Here are memories of the great fast, of the Baptism and the voice from the heavens; here is Mount Nebo, whence Moses saw the Promised Land from afar; here is Machaerus, with the head of John the Baptist lying in its plate as in a halo; here are the caves

---

[13] Titus (A.D. 39-81) was son of the Roman emperor Vespasian (A.D. 69-79) and was emperor himself from 79 to 81. Under his father's leadership, he captured Jerusalem and destroyed the Temple during the revolt of A.D. 66 to 70, known as the "Jewish War." Cestius Gallus was the governor of the Roman province of Syria at the time of the Jewish War.

[14] De Bouillon (c. A.D. 1060-1100) was the first Crusader king of Jerusalem.

[15] Babylonian king (605-562 B.C.) who conquered Judea and Jerusalem and deported the Jewish population to Babylon in the years 597-581 B.C. These events are recounted in the historical biblical books of 4 Kings, and 1 and 2 Paralipomenon, and in Jeremiah (RSV = 2 Kings, 1 and 2 Chronicles, and Jeremiah).

[16] Kings of Assyria from, respectively, 705-681 B.C. and 745-725 B.C., both of whom achieved hegemony over Israel during their reigns as recounted in 4 Kings (RSV = 2 Kings).

which gave refuge to the scapegoat, hunted for the crimes of Israel as Jesus is for ours.

Nearer, and still due east, is Mount Moriah, the pedestal of the Temple, with its southward extension bordered by the Tyropoeon Valley and the valley of Jehoshaphat, the site of the "City of David." On the horizon of this strip of immortal land is the village of Siloam, the ancient burial place of the Jews, and behind it was the Mount of Scandal, where the ancient "abominations" were perpetrated.[17]

To the west, high hills close in the view, hills that lead up to what today is called Mount Zion, and bound the curving valley of Hinnom, or Gehenna.

Such is the place where Jesus went to meet His death.

At the moment the prospect was fair and pleasing; but we know that soon a dark cloud spread over the earth. During spring in the Holy Land night often falls suddenly after hours of radiant sunshine. When the dreaded wind of the desert blows, the smoky clouds gather, beaten up by the heavy wings of the demon of the Assyrian Styx, and in the heights a war is waged between the west wind, damp and cool, and the warm breath of the Negeb. And for a time darkness reigns: an image of what befell, by an intervention of Divine Providence, at the moment of the great death.

And here is the Cross. It is a square-hewn beam, with a crosspiece. It is probably ten feet high; Rome likes to make an exhibition of her condemned criminals, for the sake of example. Jesus alludes to this when He says, "If I be lifted up from the earth

---

[17] 3 Kings 11:5-8 (RSV = 1 Kings 11:5-8).

I will draw all things to myself."[18] What is intended for His infamy He makes an instrument of glory.

The length of the beam had to be limited because it had to be thick, and yet the criminal must carry it. Therefore there had to be a limit to the weight. Moreover, certain conditions were imposed by the demands of balance and handling. It was possible to engage the shoulder against the crosspiece; but to drag the wood on the ground behind would have been out of the question.

The gibbet was probably provided with a wooden projection at some height above its base. This structure, the *antenna*, formed a sort of saddle and was designed to prevent the hands and feet from being torn under the weight of the body. However, this detail is not certain.[19]

The feet of Christ are sometimes represented as resting upon a sloping footrest. This is a pious invention for which there is no authority. Jesus must have been nailed with His legs drawn up high enough for His feet to rest flat against the beam: a frightful position, but for that very reason the more probable.

What kind of tree was privileged to provide the wood upon which the world's most precious fruit should hang? It is not certain. In all probability it was a coniferous tree. A legend fixes a valley to the southwest of the city, belonging to the Greek monastery of the Holy Cross, as the place where the tree was cut; but so many childish legends flourish in that place that it is difficult to take this seriously. As a matter of fact, it is hard to see how anyone

---

[18] John 12:32.

[19] The use of this accessory gave rise to the gruesome expression "to ride on the cross" (*equitare crucem*).

can be certain on this point. A praetorium contained a whole collection of crosses, but they bore no labels to indicate the place from which they came.

In fact, the Liturgy is better inspired when it abstracts from the material origin of a wood which is so permeated with spiritual significance:

> Faithful Cross, O tree all beauteous,
> Tree all peerless and divine,
> Not a grove on earth can show us
> Such a flower and leaf as thine.
> Sweet the nails and sweet the wood
> Laden with so sweet a load.[20]

These tender mystical reflections have a greater charm than any stories of Lot planting a tree, and of the Queen of Sheba finding the tree used to make a threshold in the temple of Solomon, and similar fantasies.

When we speak of the Cross as a piece of wood, we do not think of its growth nor of its situation. Its situation is the universe; its growth dates from the "Sixth Day," unless you would rather say that it exists and grows in the heart of the Christian when he unites himself to his divine Master. The Cross is necessary for the salvation of the world: happy the land, happy the soul willing to pay the price of it!

∞

Having established the site of Calvary and described the Cross, the question still remains, in what direction was the Sufferer

---

[20] "Crux fidelis" (traditional hymn for Good Friday).

facing? There are mystical authors who orient the Cross to the west — that is to say, they "disorient" it. Their idea is that the look which regenerates is turned toward us, Israel and the Old Law being forsaken. This theory, besides being *a priori* and not free from partiality, finds no confirmation in the situation of Calvary.

As you pass out of the Gate of Ephraim you are facing Mount Gareb, of which Calvary is a small foothill: to turn the gibbet to the west would be to make it face the hills and to hide it from the people. The idlers of the gate and the loiterers of the esplanade, the passersby who met in great numbers at the crossroads, the folk that clustered everywhere about, the dwellers in the tents set up in the open air for the feast, all these would have been foiled. The public example made of the victim would have been thwarted; furthermore, the erection of the gibbet and the management of the execution would have been made difficult. In every way, it would have been a bad arrangement.

No, Jesus faced the gate by which He had come forth, through which came His insulters and those who were greedy for a spectacle. He offered Himself to those who hated and mocked Him. He lent Himself to the convenience of His executioners.

And, if reasons of appropriateness must be added, the new Man looked toward the beginnings, toward that end of the earth from which came civilization together with the light. He faced as the apse of a church faces, having before His eyes the rampart of a world beyond which He had passed, although He had not forsaken it. His final glance saluted the Temple, His Father's house, and the rising sun.

∞

And so now the Cross is erected in its proper place, facing in the right direction, according to all the rules. The chalky soil offers a good grip; the beam holds; and now the inscription surmounts the gibbet. He who is to die has been stripped of His garments, first bound to the Cross, and then nailed to it. His crown has been left upon His head, presumably intended as a commentary upon the derisive inscription, but in truth consecrating Jesus as king of hearts and king of the universe.

The first spasms shake the body already mercilessly torn by the scourging and by a night of torment; the victim has been raised roughly upon His gibbet; the blood flows in thin streams from His hands and feet, oozes from His forehead, and stripes His breast and members along the marks of the lashes. The cruelly strained position allows no movement but the soul is unfettered, and the great shudders that rack the body leave the mind in full possession of its powers.

There is still a little more of this great life to be lived, a life which in the narrow confines of Judea embraces all the world: a cry or two more, a few more words of sovereign power, and one more lament that asks compassion of earth and Heaven: of earth, to recompense it with mercy to us, of Heaven, to grant us its blessings. And through it all is that glance which sees beyond all things, that glance which we shall follow as far as our sight can reach. But it goes infinitely beyond our vision, for it passes through the visible and invisible worlds and penetrates to their source, to the very depths of God.

∝∞∝

After the Cross has been erected, Calvary stands still for a moment, shocked into immobility by the spectacle of supreme pain. The inevitable reaction affects even the executioners. But above all it affects the Sufferer. After the terrible jolt with which the Cross fell into the rocky hole, sending a shudder through the beam and through the members of the victim, the Crucified welcomes as a sort of relief the dull, continuous agony which now ensues and will only later reach its paroxysm.

The noises of the city make themselves heard fitfully through this furtive silence. The cries of donkey drivers fill the void left by the silenced blasphemers. Camels pass with majestic tread, carrying their loads back to Jaffa or Damascus. Off in the distance the wind raises arid clouds from the sandhills. Moab is shrouded in a mist of mauve. The fig trees give forth their honeyed scent. At the foot of the Cross the red blossoms slowly increase and multiply. The hand of death, for a moment hesitating, relaxes its pitiless hold on the breast of Jesus.

∞

And then, the Master opens His eyes . . . .

2

Zion

Everything that meets His first glance speaks to Jesus of His Father's work and of the beginnings of His own. One place, a place full of mystery, especially attracts and holds His attention, for it provided a starting point in the course of ages.

Beyond the ramparts and esplanade of the Temple, between the present mosque El-Aksa and Gehenna, is a steep narrow strip of land called Ophel ("hill" or "mound"). It occupied an area of about twenty acres, twelve of which extended from the foot of the hill to Gihon, the present Fountain of the Virgin. This last piece of land, or the chief part of it, which formed a citadel, had a name three thousand years ago which was destined to reach to the ends of the earth, and, according to one of the meanings attached to it, was to have an eternal significance. This place was called *Zion*.

Yes, the "City of David," as it was called after Joab's exploit,[21] the "metropolis of the King of ages," as St. John Chrysostom called

---

[21] 1 Paralip. 11:4-7 (RSV = 1 Chron. 11:4-7).

it later, was less than two hundred yards wide in its inner enclosure. Its only water supply was the spring of Gihon, and to ensure
that in case of siege this indispensable fountain, situated outside
its borders, would not be cut off, a *sinnor*, or secret channel, had
been bored. It was by this channel that a single man, lured by
David's promises, succeeded in capturing the tiny "impregnable"
fortress.[22]

It is sometimes a very little thing that bears a great name. The
name of Zion belonged at first only to this small citadel, but was
later extended to the town — if, indeed, you could give the title
of "town" to five acres of land covered by a heap of huts that were
indistinguishable from the slopes on which they were erected, a
number of grey hovels on grey earth, an anthill without the glory
of a meadow.

The reader need not be surprised or disappointed. Life in those
far-off days, and in those regions even today, is not what our
western civilization leads us to imagine. People here live in the
open air; they meet at the gate to transact their business; they
disperse to their work on the slopes or in the valley; they sleep
beneath the stars or in the shelter of a rock, in natural caves or
even in old tombs. Only occasionally do they enter their houses,
unless the weather is bad, and then they shut themselves in.

Accommodation in the modern sense of the word is provided
only for the social authorities and for the divinity. These occupy
the citadel, which is at one and the same time a temple and a
palace. Under such conditions little space is needed. When nature
is favorable and lends herself to the convenience of human beings,
as she does in these parts, you regard your house less as a dwelling
place than as a refuge. The country is open; and so the hut, being

---

[22] 2 Kings 5:8-9 (RSV = 2 Sam. 5:8-9).

little used, is reduced to the minimum. The desert is wide; and so the lion's den need only be small.

∞

Behold, then, Master! Behold the land in which was planted the root of Jesse from which You were to come forth. See it now, humbled and hidden beneath the magnificent constructions of Herod.[23] The history that began there was to have no end; in its course it would take up Your Cross to carry it to the ends of the earth, and even to God Himself. We make the sign of the Cross in the name of the Father and of the Son and of the Holy Spirit; the Cross sets the world's history into the course of God's.

Truly that little hill has a greatness all its own, like David's gesture, that childish cast of the sling to which a giant succumbed.[24] From Zion, a point almost without extension, a vibration was to be set up that would eventually fill the whole of space and time.

Greatness is not measured only by dimensions. The Parthenon, Agrippa's Pantheon, the Cour des Lions, the Sainte Chapelle, take up very little space. Pascal's *Pensées* occupy little room on a bookshelf. Sanzio's *Vision of Ezechiel* is a canvas not more than fourteen inches square. Zion, from the moment that the Son of Man is foretold there, from the moment that the Cross with its tender burden casts its shadow upon her, becomes the city of the universe and the focus of religious hearts in all ages.

Little land greater than the world, you contain and give us eternity!

---

[23] Commonly known as "the Great," Herod was a client king of the Romans who ruled Judea from 37 B.C. to A.D. 4.

[24] 1 Kings 17 (RSV = 1 Sam. 17).

∽

From any point in the city of David, dominated by Mount Moriah and the terraces of Solomon, it was possible to see the house of Yahweh, just as from the foot of an Alpine glacier you can see the lofty peaks that crown it with towers. Of Zion the pious Israelite used to say, "God is in the midst thereof."[25] And as its conquest by the son of Jesse had caused it to be called the city of David, so Zion's conquest by Yahweh gave it the name of the City of God. Hence the Psalmist joyfully exclaimed, "With the joy of the whole earth is Mount Zion founded, on the sides of the north, the city of the Great King."[26]

∽

Israel is conscious of being the people of God, enriched with promises which she ill understands, which she often interprets in a material sense, although chosen souls — and at times even those of the poorer sort — perceive their spiritual meaning.

This is the key to the history of Israel, the paradoxical history of a tiny people that radiates power over the entire human race. Even the unbeliever finds it hard to elude the mystery of Israel. It is a story traversed by a current, and directed to a goal unknown. It knows not whither it goes, but as it goes it tells us whither it is tending, yet not knowing the meaning of what it foretells. In this history a humble event assumes a moral significance so lofty that it becomes an eternal symbol. In it Heaven and earth meet unceasingly; the childish and the cruel that we meet at every turn are allied with the sublime and the miraculous. And even when to all

[25] Ps. 45:6 (RSV = Ps. 46:5).
[26] Ps. 47:3 (RSV = Ps. 48:2).

appearance it is sunk in the depths of horror, the history of Israel is a "sacred history."

Every kind of contradiction will be found in this series of events, because these antinomies are inherent in the human principle which God is using as His instrument and whose nature He does not change.

A people at once fearless, turbulent, restless, violent, and weak; a nation of idealists and a nation of rebels; a nation of merchants and priests, of small moneylenders and heroes; a people enslaved and kingly; creatures of routine yet pioneers of new lands; realists yet in quest of an Eden; narrow and worldwide; sordid yet protectors of the poor; mean yet superhumanly proud; prophetic yet killing the prophets; venerating their oracles yet slaying those who uttered them; faithless in the name of an inflexible faith in their destiny; many times friends to their slaughterers and slaughterers of their friends: such are the people of Israel.

With a firm and tenacious belief in her high mission, Israel is false to it again and again. Indomitable to the point of heroism, none can be more servile or abject in submission. Israel is essentially a conservative people. She does not develop; she says always the same things, makes always the same gestures. She will string contradictory statements together rather than lose a single sentence of her books. She uses always the same rites, private and public, and is guided by the same few sentiments. And yet she believes in a golden age to come. While others see it only in the past, Israel sees a golden age in the future as well; and that hope is the inspiration of her heroic deeds and of her song.

Israel is the custodian of monotheism. Yet she is constantly falling into idolatry, and toying with those very cults of neighboring peoples which she has scourged with her prophecies, conscious that her national and moral salvation depends on Yahweh alone. From the time of king Solomon, out of servility to that sensual monarch, Israel tolerated centers of pagan worship near her place of burial. The Mount of Scandal is a proof of it to this very day. There, despite the repeated protests of the prophets, were the sacred gardens with their prayer slabs, their ritual trees, and niches in the rock to receive the pagan images.[27]

Yet notwithstanding pantheists, polytheists, and fetishists on every side, Israel preserved her faith in the one true God. She transmitted that faith intact to posterity. Her very prevarications only served to emphasize the mission she had to fulfill, only called forth from her spokesmen clearer and more definite pronounce-ments. She promulgated the Law, the promises, and the hopes. Conscious of the covenant, breaking it and renewing it, and finally unfaithful, Israel is the mediator of an eternal pact that, absorbing her in the rest of humanity, is destined to embrace the whole world.

ↂ

It is a remarkable fact that the whole of the history of the Cross and its consequences is written in the Hebrew books. Zion is not only the place of preparation; it is also the place of prophecy. Israel foresees and foretells; her religious genius has a spirit that is unshackled by the bonds of time, and her Yahweh speaks close to her ear.

Under the pen of the prophets, psalmists, chroniclers, sages, and lawgivers, the history of this day, and of the eternal day that is its outcome, is anticipated and set forth sentence by sentence, phrase by phrase, without apparent coherence or plan, yet in such a manner that when the event happens, recalling these memories

----

[27] 3 Kings 11:5-8 (RSV = 1 Kings 11:5-8); 4 Kings 23:13-14 (RSV = 2 Kings 23:13-14).

and coordinating them, there arises a complete and striking description to vindicate those voices of long ago.

The coming of the Messiah, His characteristics, His work, His life and death, His Resurrection, His glory, His eternal rule over the elect, are described clearly in a few rapid sentences. Some texts will suffice in illustration:

> "The scepter shall not be taken away from Judah,
> nor a ruler from his thigh, till He comes that is to be sent:
> and He shall be the expectation of nations."[28]

> "And thou, Bethlehem Ephrata, art a little one among
> the thousands of Judah: out of thee shall He come forth unto
> me that is to be the ruler in Israel; and His going forth is from
> the beginning, from the days of eternity."[29]

> "A virgin shall conceive and bear a son; and His
> name shall be called Emmanuel (God with us)."[30]

> "For a child is born to us, and a son is given to us, and the
> government is upon His shoulder; and His name shall be
> called Wonderful, Counselor, God the Mighty, the Father
> of the world to come, the Prince of Peace."[31]

> "Behold I send my angel and he shall prepare the way
> before my face. And presently the Lord whom you seek,
> and the angel of the testament whom you desire, shall come
> to His temple. Behold He cometh."[32]

[28] Gen. 49:10.
[29] Mic. 5:2.
[30] Isa. 7:14.
[31] Isa. 9:6.
[32] Mal. 3:1.

"The people that walked in darkness,
have seen a great light."[33]

"Then shall the eyes of the blind be opened, and the ears of
the deaf shall be unstopped. Then shall the lame man leap as
a hart, and the tongue of the dumb shall be free."[34]

"Behold my servant, I will uphold Him. My elect, my soul
delighteth in Him. I have given my spirit upon Him, He shall
bring forth judgment to the Gentiles. He shall not cry, nor
have respect to person, neither shall His voice be heard
abroad. The bruised reed He shall not break, and
smoking flax He shall not quench."[35]

"Rejoice greatly, O daughter of Zion, shout for joy,
O daughter of Jerusalem: behold thy king will come to thee,
the just and Savior: He is poor, and riding upon an ass,
and upon a colt, the foal of an ass."[36]

"For even the man of my peace, in whom I trusted,
who ate my bread, hath greatly supplanted me."[37]

"And they weighed for my wages thirty pieces of silver.
And the Lord said to me: Cast it to the statuary, a handsome
price, that I was prized at by them. And I took the thirty
pieces of silver, and I cast them into the house of
the Lord to the statuary."[38]

---

[33] Isa. 9:2.
[34] Isa. 35:5-6.
[35] Isa. 42:1-3.
[36] Zech. 9:9.
[37] Ps. 40:10 (RSV = Ps. 41:9).
[38] Zech. 11:12-13.

"Unjust witnesses rising up have asked me things
that I knew not. They repaid me evil for good."[39]

"I gave my body to the strikers, and my cheeks to those
who plucked them: I did not turn my face from those who
rebuked me, and spit upon me."[40]

"They gave me gall for my food, and in my thirst
they gave me vinegar to drink."[41]

"All they that saw me have laughed me to scorn:
they have spoken with the lips and wagged the head.
He hoped in the Lord, let Him deliver him: let Him save him,
seeing He delighteth in him. . . . I am poured out like water;
and all my bones are scattered. . . . The council of the
malignant hath besieged me. They have dug my hands
and feet. They have numbered all my bones. And they
have looked and stared upon me. They have parted
my garments amongst them; and upon my
vesture they cast lots."[42]

"Surely He hath borne our infirmities and carried
our sorrows: and we have thought Him as it were a leper,
and as one struck by God and afflicted. But He was wounded
for our iniquities, and He was bruised for our sins:
the chastisement of our peace was upon Him;
and by His bruises we are healed."[43]

---

[39] Ps. 34:11-12 (RSV = Ps. 35:11-12).

[40] Isa. 50:6.

[41] Ps. 68:22 (RSV = 69:21).

[42] Ps. 21:8-19 (RSV = Ps. 22:7-18).

[43] Isa. 53:4-5.

*"Thou wilt not leave my soul in Hell; nor wilt Thou
give Thy Holy One to see corruption. Thou wilt make
known to me the ways of life."*[44]

*"Sit Thou at my right hand, until I make
Thy enemies Thy footstool."*[45]

*"Therefore will I distribute to Him very many,
and He shall divide the spoils of the strong, because
He hath delivered His soul unto death, and was
reputed with the wicked."*[46]

*"Arise, be enlightened, O Jerusalem; for thy light is come,
and the glory of the Lord is risen upon thee. For behold darkness shall cover the earth, and a mist the people: but the Lord
shall arise upon thee, and His glory shall be seen upon thee.
And the Gentiles shall walk in thy light, and kings in the brightness of thy rising. Lift up thy eyes round about, and see: all
these are gathered together, they are come to thee."*[47]

*"I beheld therefore in the vision of the night,
and lo, one like the Son of Man came with the clouds
of Heaven, and He came even to the Ancient of Days:
and they presented Him before Him. And He gave Him
power, and glory, and a kingdom: and all peoples, tribes,
and tongues shall serve Him: His power is an everlasting
power that shall not be taken away: and His kingdom
shall not be destroyed."*[48]

---

[44] Ps. 15:10-11 (RSV = Ps. 16:10-11).

[45] Ps. 109:1 (RSV = Ps. 110:1).

[46] Isa. 53:12.

[47] Isa. 60:1-4.

[48] Dan. 7:13-14.

It is certain that Jesus thought of these things as He hung upon the Cross. His cry of anguish, "My God, my God, why hast Thou forsaken me?" is the first sentence of a long prophetic Psalm from which several of the above passages have been taken.[49] Jesus lives upon these ancient prophecies. He proclaims them; He comments upon them in the synagogues; He explains them to His disciples; and at Emmaus He weaves them all into one discourse.

And just as He associates Himself with the prophecies of which His mission is the fulfillment, so also He gazes forward into the mysteries of the future. The time that is to come appears to Him as though it were present. Both past and future meet Him as He walks His path, for His path is set in eternity. All that He has to do and to suffer is already written in the book of God, and men also had written it on earth. But the consequences that are to come are no less foreseen. These, too, He sees with the seers; and in His turn He prophesies what is to come.

This has been represented by the artist James Tissot, who depicts Christ on the Cross as raised in a sort of ecstasy. Around Him in a circle are the ancient prophets, scrolls in hand, and among them those two who appeared in the cloud of Mount Tabor, discussing with Him the event that was shortly to be accomplished. These witnesses seem to say, "Lo, the event coincides with the word; time keeps faith with time; Providence speaks and fulfills; God comes to meet God."

And now Jesus looks with tenderness upon Zion, that mysterious link between two worlds, Zion that is so humbled now and already perhaps a little forlorn.

He sees there His first beginnings, for Zion was the cradle of His race. In the conqueror and ruler of that little land of symbols,

---

[49] Ps. 21:1 (RSV = Ps. 22:1).

in the vanquisher of Goliath, in the sorrowful and merciful father of Absalom, in the zealous promoter of divine worship and the sublime spokesman of religious souls in every age, He sees the type of Himself as the everlasting spiritual King.

At the two extremities of that genealogical tree whose fruit is the Cross there stand David and Jesus, the type and the fulfillment, the sacrifice foretold and the sacrifice accomplished. That which the joyous Psalmist announces in exultation, Christ fulfills in pain.

3

His Father's House

If every devout Israelite in contemplating Jerusalem saw only the Temple, then we must believe that Jesus, zealous as He was for His Father's honor and ever prostrate in adoration before Him, gazed from His Cross at the house of His Father in a spirit of ardent worship, mingled with unspeakable sorrow.

His Cross was situated to the west and His face was turned almost in exactly the same direction as the Temple, of which He thus saw only the back. Given the season of the year and the time of day, the shadow of the Cross would, if extended, have covered the sacred edifice and the altar beyond. These striking calculations may easily be verified on the spot; they are no fruit of the imagination. Fantasy on this subject would be out of place.

Now that the altar of the universe is erected, and the real victim so often typified in the sacrifices of the Temple at last installed on it, the shadow reaches forth and joins the ancient figures. What in the Temple had been hidden and hedged around with symbols, on the Cross now stands unveiled. What had been foretold in mystery is now made manifest to the world. The prelude dies away to a silence which heralds the eternal canticle. The religious stronghold of Israel, which to this day stands high in the divine history of the world, yields slowly to the weight of the humble and irresistible Cross.

It might be supposed that this city of the Great King, which for Him has become a city of death and for the religious universe a city of ruin, arouses in His heart now only feelings of aversion and contempt. Some have been of this opinion. According to them the sublime Shepherd now repudiates the spot where His sheep-fold was first established; the New Testament repudiates the Old which was its root; God in the person of Yahweh is renounced by God in the person of Christ. Away with these delusions!

It is true that the Temple is condemned, the Law abrogated; the West is now to replace the East in much of the part that it played. But can Jesus forget that this corner of earth, faithless though it has proven and guilty even of deicide, has nevertheless for upwards of a thousand years been "the tabernacle of God in the midst of men,"[50] the palladium of the human race, and a divinely appointed shelter for humanity in its onward march to destiny?

And He Himself, the Son of Man, does He owe nothing to this place of worship to which He has wended His way so often since His earliest years, where He gave His first lesson at the age of twelve, where He fulfilled the Law to the letter, beginning with the day when His mother in obedience to that Law carried Him to the Gate of Nicanor, and made Him ascend those fifteen circular steps to redeem His tender young life with a pair of doves?

How many times has Jesus walked under the porch of Solomon, whose glistening columns He now sees before Him, its pavement sparkling in the midday sun! It was there that He taught "with

---

[50] Cf. Wis. of Sol. 9:8.

authority,"[51] accosting groups, welcoming questions, or confuting the arguments of the doctors. There He would sit sometimes on the ground, His hearers gathered around Him, after the manner of the rabbis. Or He would go and take His place in the Court of the Women, close by the treasury where offerings to the Temple were made, where the *Sanhedrists*[52] would pass on their way to the council chamber, followed sometimes by an accused person, like the adulterous woman whom He delivered from her fate.

Jesus prayed with fervor in the holy place of His people. Did He not define the Temple as a "house of prayer"?[53] Had He not "gone up"[54] to all the great feasts, to "pay His vows to the Most High"?[55] Like all the Jews, Jesus saw in the Temple an image of Heaven. He gave it the same name: when He spoke of "His Father's house"[56] one could not know immediately whether He meant His eternal dwelling place or His temporal and earthly abode.

The episode of the sellers whom He drove out of the Temple, regarded by some as merely an angry gesture, is indeed due to anger, but to a loving anger, whose source lay in respect for His Father.[57] He who had come to the Temple ordinarily as a teacher, on that day came as judge and master. But why purify this domain and set it in order, if not because He loved it? Let there be no doubt: Jesus loved this Tabor of stone where His Father had

---

[51] Matt. 7:29; Mark 1:22; Luke 4:32.

[52] That is, members of the *Sanhedrin*, the supreme court of chief priests and elders in Jerusalem empowered to pass judgment on a variety of civil and religious matters concerning the Jewish population.

[53] Matt. 21:13; Mark 11:17; Luke 19:46.

[54] Cf. Luke 2:42.

[55] Cf. Ps. 49:14 (RSV = Ps. 50:14).

[56] John 2:16, 14:2.

[57] Matt. 21:12-13; Mark 11:15-17; Luke 19:45-48; John 2:13-17.

appeared in glory to the eyes of thirty generations, as He Himself had appeared on the sacred Mount.[58]

These stones gilded by the long hours of sunshine, these copper plates made green by the torrential rains and then dyed russet brown by the heats of summer, are beautiful in the eyes of Jesus, as they are in the eyes of the fortunate pilgrim who has come up for the Passover. Their splendor stirs Him to grief. He would gladly cast over them a veil of mourning such as we cast over the Cross on Good Friday. He loves them and is sad, for He cannot but contrast the proud majesty of today with the humiliation and the disaster of the morrow.

Jesus accepted the whole religious organization of His people, before rejecting it because of their impenitence. "The scribes and Pharisees," He said, "have sat on the chair of Moses. All things therefore whatsoever they shall say to you, observe and do: but according to their works do ye not."[59] And of their government, He said, "Do not think that I am come to destroy the Law or the prophets. I am not come to destroy, but to fulfill."[60]

An institution is fulfilled when it is developed, even though development may carry it beyond itself. In the state in which it was, Judaism could not endure, precisely because it was a way of approach. Its duty, when once Christ had come, was to abdicate in favor of Christ, to renew itself according to His words and His spirit, and thus to enter into a new way, but a way which should be in continuity with the old, as the larva or chrysalis is continuous with the insect into which it is transformed.

Such a transformation means death, if you will, but a glorious death, a death which is in reality a survival, in which all those

[58] That is, in the Transfiguration (Matt. 17, Mark 9, Luke 9).

[59] Matt. 23:2-3.

[60] Matt. 5:17.

souls that freely submit, all the authorities that accept the meta-morphosis, are crowned with the glory of a higher and nobler condition.

It is possible to picture Israel receiving Christ with acclama-tion, her chiefs leading the way, her priests invested with the new priesthood, her Sanhedrin becoming the Council, her doctors becoming, like Paul, teachers of the Gospel and apostles of the Gentiles. One could picture the Temple, as a result, hallowed with a new consecration and assuming a new and wider role, raised to the dignity of the first Christian church, a temple now in the fullest sense of the word: its Holy of Holies, hitherto empty with the desolation of an anteroom, the home now of the living and eternal Holy One of God.

Can we doubt that this was the ideal of Jesus Himself, during those years when He was already granting to an unconscious tabernacle the blessing of His real presence? Was not the Temple already a hallowed place, since Jesus was present in it? It had only to retain that consecration; it had only to allow the physical presence of Christ to give place to His sacramental presence, to acquiesce in an end to that series of developments in the true worship of God, which began with the stone anointed by Jacob[61] and which culminates in our Catholic altars.

And what a glorious Jerusalem would Christendom then have had! It would have lacked that note of pathos which we find in the Holy City today, but what a glory for her sons, and what an honor to the human race! No Mosque of Omar would then have been enthroned upon the esplanade of Solomon. The sacred porches of the Temple would have been the scene of processions of the Blessed Sacrament; and in the place where once the smoke of

---

[61] Gen. 28:18.

sacrifice blackened the altars we should have seen clouds of sweet-smelling incense.

For evidently in such a case Jerusalem would never have been destroyed. Her fall had been clearly foretold as a sanction of Divine Providence. The "hen" would have gathered her chickens under her wing and would have defended them,[62] and neither Roman eagle nor any of the vultures who came searching for prey in the wake of her triumph could ever have borne them away.

But alas! Like so many other religious and political authorities, Jerusalem refused to yield. She failed, with the exception of some few of her sons devoid of social prestige, to know "the things that were to her peace,"[63] and she fell a victim to the foreign invader. Her refusal to develop was the signature of her doom. The God who had dwelt there in symbol deigned to come in His own person. But now that He is rejected, this house of God will be in very truth a house of desolation, yielded to destruction. He who drives God forth is destined to perish.

As Jesus hangs there dying and beholds this Temple, which is also dying, does He not go back in His mind over its past history, as dying people are wont to do? And what a long history it is that will come to an end with the destruction of this famous Temple, which no less than three times has risen under different forms to a new life! There was the Temple of Solomon which David had dreamed of building.[64] Then came the Temple of Zerubbabel built

---

[62] Matt. 23:37; Luke 13:34.

[63] Luke 19:42.

[64] Solomon was the son of David, who reigned for forty years in the second third of the tenth century B.C.

after the captivity,[65] and now, finally, there is this Temple of Herod the Great, constructed at the moment when Israel, already the captive of Rome, is soon to become the slave of all. The Temple is the symbol of Israel in all its phases of glory and humiliation, of loyalty and crime.

When the ancient city of Jebus became the city of David it saw an immediate change in the religious regime of Israel, which until then had enjoyed little stability. Yahweh had hitherto been content with a portable sanctuary, the sacred Tent or "Tabernacle," also called the "Tent of Union" (of Yahweh with his people) or the "Tent of Testimony," because of the tables of the Law which reposed in it.

But now that Israel was firmly established in her capital, now that the king himself had a house of cedarwood, it ill befitted Yahweh to dwell in Jerusalem as a wanderer. The ancient Tabernacle must take up its fixed abode upon the mountain and by its own stability ensure the stable condition of the people.

And so David sought out the "high place" upon which the new sanctuary should be erected. He purchased the threshing floor of Ornan the Jebusite and set up an altar on it immediately.[66]

This was already an advance upon early Semitic sanctuaries. The ancient Semites contented themselves with a *haram*, or sacred enclosure, carefully marked off as the property of the god, usually surrounded by a low wall or hedge, and there without further ado they would set up their sacred stone. The place would doubtless be characterized by some natural peculiarity, such as rising ground, a spring, or a remarkable tree; but there was nothing

---

[65] Zerubbabel appears with Jeshua the high priest as the recipient of Haggai's call (Hag. 1:1) to rebuild the Temple after the return of the Jewish exiles from the Babylonian Captivity (sixth century B.C.).

[66] 1 Paralip. 21:15-26 (RSV = 1 Chron. 21:15-26).

architectural about the installation. The erection of an altar was a first step toward the building of an edifice designed to shelter it.

At the time when David was preparing the threshing floor of Ornan, the Tabernacle and the altar of holocausts were at Gibeon. The Ark of the Covenant was at Jerusalem in its temporary tent. It was not until 1013 B.C., during the reign of Solomon, that the prophecy of Nathan[67] would be fulfilled and a start made on building the first Temple.

Solomon had not the means at his disposal for building a great monument. He had gold and cattle; he had his harvests and he had his pride; but he had no first-class materials, no skillful workmen, and not the least notion of art. He therefore had recourse to the Tyrians, who possessed all the necessary resources and in their architectural conceptions combined the art of Egypt with that of Assyria.

Within seven years[68] the house of Yahweh was completed. Like the Egyptian temples, its essential features were a *vestibule* or pylon, an outer sanctuary (the "Holy"), and an inner and more sacred sanctuary (the "Holy of Holies"), which none might enter, save the high priest once a year. A number of additional chambers were set apart for the service of the Temple, while the whole was to be surrounded by a number of pillared porches, which were completed only at a much later date.

Under the *haram* of Solomon cisterns had been dug to serve the needs of the personnel and for use in the sacrifices. For washing purposes a large bronze basin (called "The Sea of Bronze") had been provided, in imitation of the *piscinas*, or pools, of Susa.[69]

---

[67] 1 Paralip. 17 (RSV = 1 Chron. 17).

[68] By 1006 B.C.

[69] Susa was the capital of the Persian empire under Darius I (522-486 B.C.) and his successors. It was conquered by Alexander in 331 B.C.

.   And finally the sovereign, with the queen, took up residence by the side of his God.

∞

Although it was one day to be surpassed, the work thus completed by Solomon was magnificent. We should note that the measurements of the building were in no way arbitrary: they correspond to that symbolism of numbers which, together with the symbolism of forms and words, was popular among the Egyptians. The dimensions adopted for the various parts of the edifice were like the elements of an arithmetical problem, to which the whole provided the solution. The side elevation was based upon the equilateral triangle and the front upon the right-angled triangle, which was, according to Plato, the perfect and most beautiful of all triangles, its sides represented by the numbers 3, 4, and 5.

The decoration consisted of carved panelling overlaid with plates of gold, according to the Babylonian usage. Coverings of cedar and cypress wood were used throughout, including the pavements. There were sacred vessels almost entirely of gold, as well as tables for the offerings, candlesticks, winged cherubim carved in wood and plated with gold, and other objects lavishly adorned.

This building lasted without alteration for a little more than four centuries; and the Israelite took in it a pride which we can hardly conceive. He saw in it "the joy of the whole earth,"[70] and the devout combined with their national pride a feeling of happiness at seeing their God so glorified. Thus they readily identified their love of the Temple with their devotion to God Himself:

[70] Ps. 47:3 (RSV = Ps. 48:2).

"How beautiful are Thy tabernacles, O Lord of hosts! My soul longeth and fainteth for the courts of the Lord. My heart and my flesh have rejoiced in the living God."[71]

But in the year 588 B.C. the wondrous sanctuary was desecrated and destroyed by Nebuchadnezzar, the king of Chaldea. Fifty-two years later the deliverance of Jerusalem by Cyrus[72] enabled Zerubbabel to raise it from its ruins. Its reconstruction on a smaller scale, but on the original foundations, took twenty years (536-516 B.C.), and it was not until 445 B.C. that the rampart was rebuilt by Nehemiah.[73]

∞

This was the state of the Temple when Pompey[74] captured Jerusalem and Herod came to install himself in the city. The murdering usurper had so many sins to expiate that he sought by every possible means to conciliate the Jewish people, and especially the priestly caste. He devoted nearly three years to collecting the necessary materials. He fixed upon a plan which enshrined the original arrangement of the building and to a certain extent reproduced its style, although with predominantly Graeco-Roman technique.

When all was ready, Herod set to work. Ten thousand workmen were employed upon the building, under the supervision of a thousand priests, these alone being allowed to work in the "Holy" and in the "Holy of Holies." Within eighteen months the *naos*, or

---

[71] Ps. 83:2-3 (RSV = Ps. 84:1-2).

[72] Persian emperor and ruler of the Babylonian empire (539-530 B.C.).

[73] Jewish governor active in the fifth century B.C. and subject of the biblical book of the same name.

[74] Roman general who captured Jerusalem in 63 B.C.

sanctuary proper, was completed and dedicated. Eight years were then devoted to constructing the precincts and the porches, while incidental work lasted until A.D. 64, the time of Agrippa[75] — that is to say, until the eve of its total destruction.

Herod's Temple, considered as a whole, is the embodiment of a fine architectural conception: concentric cloisters or colonnades surround the mountain one above the other, culminating in the sanctuary itself which occupies the summit of the rock.

Seen from a distance and in a favorable light, its effect is marvelous. The white marble of the walls, embellished with silver and gold, seems like sparkling snow. The view from the Mount of Olives at sunrise is dazzling: the gilded roofs, the gates, the orna-ments, and the gigantic vine of pure gold before the gate of the Basilica glisten in the sun. At the sight of it, the heart of an Israelite pilgrim glows with pride, as he murmurs to himself the words of the Psalm: "Out of Zion the loveliness of God's beauty shall come."[76]

But when the people from all parts come up in their crowds for the great feasts, pressing through the gates and filling the courts; when the priests fulfill their office and hurry to and fro; when the learned doctors hold their discussions, surrounded by groups of habitual or occasional disciples; when the Sanhedrin deliberates; when through the porches oxen, sheep, goats, and lambs are led in for the sacrifice; when lepers come to be cleansed and anxious husbands bring their wives to submit them to the test of the "water of bitterness";[77] when money changers and sellers of doves and cakes conduct their noisy business — it is then that this great

---

[75] Herod Agrippa II, died A.D. 100, descendant of Herod the Great.

[76] Ps. 49:2-3 (RSV = Ps. 50:2-3).

[77] This refers to a type of trial by ordeal (as described in Numbers 5) to determine whether a wife has committed adultery in secret.

structure becomes intensely alive, the vital expression of all that it represents.

The whole of this mighty place is then filled with the crackling of fire, the screams of animals, the sound of voices, footsteps, and the blare of sacred trumpets. The Temple's true foundation is not Haram or Moriah; it is not Jerusalem nor even the Holy Land. It is the whole Jewish world, whether at home or abroad, which finds in this sanctuary its spiritual summit, its religious, civic, political, economic, and intellectual citadel.

Haggai had said of the second Temple, "Great shall be the glory of this last house more than of the first."[78] Herod thought to fulfill this part of the prophecy himself. But the prophet had added, "And in this place I will give peace."[79] In this respect the prophecy is fulfilled by Jesus, and He buys our peace at the price of His pain.

∞

What are the thoughts of our suffering Savior as He gazes for the last time upon this great monument with all that it symbolizes and portends? This is an inexhaustible subject of surmise.

In this Temple the smoke of the adoring incense is still rising in the air, the echo of the Psalms can still be heard; the rites which had once lived a mysterious life borrowed from His are now barely dead — and Jesus repudiates it. It has accumulated riches from every resource that the nation possesses; but it has now lost its ancient religious splendor, and become a gaudy and ostentatious palace, a facade of hypocrisy. Its marble whiteness is like the whitewash splashed on tombs which hide rotting bones within. For the Pharisees it is become a center for disputes and stubborn

[78] Hag. 2:10.
[79] Ibid.

rivalry; for others it is a place of commerce and fraud, "a den of thieves."[80]

It had been founded to be the vestibule of the true Temple, just as the age in which it flourished was the vestibule of the Christian era. In resisting its fate it stands condemned.

Events had long since given their verdict. Israel had been warned. The prophets had often said what one of them proclaimed with such vigor and force. "Even so," said Jeremiah, as he violently broke a potter's vessel in the sight of the ancients and priests, "even so will I break this people, and this city, as the potter's vessel is broken which cannot be made whole again."[81]

Then came John the Baptist, crying out in the twilight between prophecy and fulfillment. "For now the ax," he said, "is laid to the root of the tree."[82]

The final admonition was given by Jesus Himself. A week before the final catastrophe He warned His disciples. The solemnity of that warning imparts to His glance now perhaps something of its sadness but also, I think, something of its gentle compassion. Is it possible to be angry, to be harsh with one who is condemned to death?

∞

It was on one of those days of wearisome discussion, after which He would retire to the peace of Bethany, that one of the Twelve called His attention to the beauties of the Temple. "See," he says, pointing to the massive building before them, "see, Master, what manner of stones and what buildings are here! Jesus answers,

[80] Matt. 21:13; Mark 11:17; Luke 19:46.
[81] Jer. 19:11.
[82] Matt. 3:10; Luke 3:9.

"Seest thou all these great buildings? There shall not be left a stone upon a stone, that shall not be thrown down."[83]

The words fall like a thunderbolt upon His astonished hearers. The Twelve are dumbfounded; without a word the little group passes down to Kedron and ascends the Mount of Olives. When they have nearly reached the summit Jesus stops, turns, and bids His disciples sit down. There, facing that rocky mountain to all appearances eternal, He strips aside the deceptive veil of glory with which the setting sun has adorned the Holy City, and takes from the Temple the crown which the bright horizon has set upon it. "Take heed," He says, "lest any man deceive you."[84] Then He foretells the end.

The description is detailed and circumstantial. His hearers are shown the drama itself with all that precedes and accompanies it; signs, events, and consequences — all are foretold. And so awesome is this thing which He prophesies that He makes it serve as a symbol of a much greater and more decisive catastrophe: the end of the world.

When this latter event will come to pass nobody knows, not even "the Son of Man",[85] but the fall of Jerusalem and the destruction of the Temple will not be long delayed: "This generation shall not pass before all these things shall be accomplished."[86] In less than forty years that naked sword, which David saw in the hands of the angel on Ornan's threshing floor,[87] will set about its deadly work, and its whirling blade will destroy all that has form and life in the rebellious city.

---

[83] Mark 13:1-2.

[84] Mark 13:5.

[85] Cf. Mark 13:32.

[86] Matt. 24:34.

[87] 1 Paralip. 21:16 (RSV = 1 Chron. 21:16).

And Jewish hands will help. The first attacks will be made during the civil war between the Seleucids and the Maccabees.[88] The Romans will come later; but then they will utterly destroy the city. Fire and pick will demolish these unshakable foundations, and the efforts of Julian the Apostate[89] to replace them will only serve to render all the more evident the fulfillment of Jesus' words: "There shall not remain a stone upon a stone."[90]

How mournfully must Jesus now look for the last time upon this scene of animation and prosperity, upon this busy city, with its noble porches and towers. He sees the day when the plain and the two long hills upon which the city stands will be a desert; when all this glittering beauty will be desolation; when what remains of Zion behind the proud basilica will seem like a city overturned, its soil above the ground and its life hidden beneath: nothing to be seen but holes, caves, and tombs — silence, ashes, death.

"I beheld the earth, and saw that it was void and nothing: and the heavens, and there was no light in them. I looked upon the mountains, and behold they trembled: and all the hills were troubled. I beheld, and lo there was no man: and all the birds of the air were gone. I looked, and behold Carmel was a wilderness: and all its cities were destroyed at the presence of the Lord, and at the presence of the wrath of His indignation."[91]

---

[88] In the second century B.C., the Jews, led by the Maccabees, revolted against the Seleucid rulers (successors to Alexander the Great) who had conquered Jerusalem. 1 Macc. 1-4 describes the first stages of the revolt. Some Jews cooperated with the attempts of the Seleucids to force paganism on the Jewish population (1 Macc. 1:11-15).

[89] Roman emperor A. D. 361-363, who rejected his Christian upbringing in favor of paganism. He proposed rebuilding the Temple in Jerusalem in a letter from early 363, but did not live to carry out this plan.

[90] Mark 13:2.

[91] Jer. 4:23-26.

Like Ai under Joshua, Jerusalem will be reduced to "a heap forever."[92] The valley below the Temple will be more than ever "the country of death,"[93] the Temple itself a great tomb surrounded by other tombs, ever spreading until they cover the neighboring hills. An eddy of tombs, waves of death, a storm of ashes. . . .

All the noise of the colonnades will be silenced. Instead of busy tumult there will be a mournful peace. Weeds will sprout between the worn paving stones of the Holy of Holies. Upon the rock where the altar of holocausts is now enthroned a Moslem mosque will rise, as if in prohibition: "Israel shall not adore where she has betrayed." Israel will bewail her fate by the ruins of the outer walls. The Wailing Wall will be her consolation, even while strangers mock this crumbling relic of the holy Zion of long ago.

And meanwhile the Crucified, who now gazes on the city with bloodshot eyes, who groans in pain, seeming at times to collapse and allow the night to descend upon His soul — meanwhile the Crucified will have become great. The Tree planted on this humble mound will have driven its roots deep into the center of the earth. Its branches will reach the heavens, and that greatness of Israel which is so soon to pass away, that material greatness which is full of deceit and treachery, will be replaced by a spiritual greatness that will bring blessings to the universe.

Jesus is the cornerstone of a new Temple "not made with hands."[94] "The stone which the builders rejected will become the cornerstone,"[95] and also "no man can lay any other foundation save that which hath been laid, which is Christ Jesus."[96]

---

[92] Josh. 8:28.
[93] Jer. 31:40.
[94] Heb. 9:11.
[95] Acts 4:11.
[96] 1 Cor. 3:11.

4

The Upper Room

"Jesus, knowing that His hour was come, that He should pass out of this world to the Father, having loved His own that were in the world, He loved them unto the end."[97]

This sublime prelude is always an appropriate introduction to any consideration of the events of Holy Thursday, and of those other events which we associate with them because they occurred in the same place.

The scene of this "end" of love was an upper room on Mount Zion, which we call the *Cenacle*,[98] directly south of Calvary, and situated to the right of Jesus as He hangs upon the Cross, at a distance of half a mile.

The earliest Christian traditions make the disciples the owners of the house in which the institution of the Eucharist and the descent of the Holy Spirit took place.

[97] John 13:1.

[98] From the Latin *cenaculum*, or "eating room," often located in the upper story of a house.

Some have wondered whether in fact both these events occurred in the same house. There is room for doubt, because the Gospel story is not explicit on the point.

Surely, however, it is enough that the account does not exclude the possibility, to make us accept it as a fact. The Passover is celebrated by Jesus and His disciples in a house where they are at home. Always sure of a welcome, they can resort to it whenever they choose. And they cannot have many such houses in Jerusalem. He who has "no place to lay His head"[99] is not constantly changing His dwelling. And, moreover, the room which once witnessed His last utterances and the most mysterious institution that the world has ever seen, will afterward possess a unique fascination for them.

Jesus wishes these two manifestations to produce a lasting impression, and one can hardly imagine that He would deliberately run the risk of weakening that impression by separating the events: the farewell banquet in one place, the banquet of posthumous thanksgiving in another; the promise of the Spirit in one place and His coming in another.

We may perhaps add as a reason the religious connection between the two occurrences. It is fitting that the institution of the Eucharist and the descent of the Holy Spirit should occur in the same place, for they are fundamentally the same thing. They are two sacraments, but they produce the same effect; they are like two breaths of the same atmosphere. The flesh and blood of Christ give life only by giving us His Spirit — "The flesh profiteth nothing"[100] — and the Spirit gives life to those who unite themselves with the body of Jesus according to His will, in that mystical unity which is the fruit of His Passover.

[99] Matt. 8:20; Luke 9:58.
[100] John 6:64.

From the point of view of the Church, too, another reason of a similar kind is given by the third-century treatise, the *Didascalia* [or "Teaching"] *of the Apostles*: "Just as in the upper room was first celebrated the mystery of the Body and Blood of our Lord (afterwards to govern the whole world), so in the upper room began the preaching of His Gospel (afterwards to rule the universe)."

∞

Here, then, far to the right of the gibbet, is that spiritual mountain beneath which the world will pitch its camp, even as the tents of Israel were set up beneath the sky in the days of the manna. The Cenacle is truly for Jesus the Bethlehem of His work, as that tiny village was the Bethlehem of His birth; the Cenacle is the second "House of Bread."[101]

There on the preceding evening the banquet of the universe was spread; from thence in a few days will go forth the power of the Spirit that sets all in motion. The invisible miracle of Holy Thursday will have been the prelude to visible wonders. But who shall say whether it is not rather the invisible wonder that will be the more marvelous in its effects? Does not God produce all His works through the human heart?

While He suffers, Jesus has no need to be concerned for the immediate future of His Church. For this, Heaven has already provided; and even now provision is being made. The bread of the future is ready; the tongues of fire glow darkly beneath the vaults of the Cenacle; the wind is but holding its mighty breath; feet are

---

[101] The Temple in Jerusalem could be called the "House of Bread" because of the twelve loaves of bread (called the "Showbread") placed on a golden table in its sanctuary as a sacrificial offering. See Exod. 25:30; 1 Kings 21:6 (RSV = 1 Sam. 21:6).

already waiting to run throughout the earth; hearts are burning to set it on fire. What powers are latent around the Cross!

Perhaps the most striking thing about the Passion is the intermingling of two currents of events, the one bearing upon the present and pushing it inexorably to the fatal climax, the other arranging the future and sowing the seeds of eternal life in the universe of souls.

While in the court of Caiaphas and in the Sanhedrin men are debating how Christ may be slain, Christ Himself, only a few yards away, devises the means whereby He may live forever on earth. In the very moment in which He seems to be captured in Judas' trap, Christ is fully master of His fate. He disposes the manner of His sacrifice and the commemoration that shall be made of it, as well as the part that each one of the faithful shall take in it for all time.

It is as though there were two independent designs. But in reality the one dominates the other, and that one is not the design of Caiaphas. There are two plans, but God's plan is not thwarted by the plan of men, for men are His instruments. Men serve His purpose, and that is the reason — says St. Leo — why Jesus does not debar Judas from the Cenacle. Under His very eyes He allows him to plan his dastardly crime. What a light this throws upon the transcendence of God's activity and upon the workings of His Providence!

Some have wondered why Jesus, seeking a place in which to eat the Passover, did not avail Himself of the house of Lazarus, where He was staying during those days. The reason was that the Passover had to be eaten in the city. From the ends of the earth Jews were journeying to Jerusalem for this purpose. Could Jesus and His disciples appear to grudge the small effort required to conform to the ancient usage?

Moreover, Jesus intended now to convey His final teaching, to make His last testament; and it was not fitting that strangers should be present, even if they were strangers who had been admitted to the closest intimacy, such as Magdalene, Martha, and Lazarus. One day when He was preaching someone had spoken to Him of His mother and His brethren. He had pointed to His disciples, saying, "Behold my mother and my brethren."[102] This sense of spiritual ties was now uppermost. The institution of the sacrifice and of the new priesthood, the promulgation of the new commandment, the promise of the Holy Spirit who should come to strengthen the Church, the final outpourings of His heart — all this called for a strict and what, for all its tenderness, might be called an *official* intimacy. Into this circle of privileged beings He admits none save those whom He has chosen as associates in His work, His friends in the ritual sense, the preachers and the bishops of the morrow.

∞

And so Jesus sends two of His disciples from the Mount of Olives into the city. There they will meet a man carrying a pitcher of water. Possibly he will recognize them; in any case they are to follow him, and having reached his lodging, they are to say to him, "The Master saith: Where is my room that I may eat the Passover with my disciples?"[103]

The room in question (in Greek, *kataluma*) is the reception room that in any important house is always reserved for guests — what we in English call the "parlor" to which travelers and visitors are admitted. In the next sentence Jesus calls it an "upper room" (*anagaion*).[104] In connection with the appearances of the risen

---

[102] Matt. 12:49; Mark 3:34.
[103] Mark 14:14.
[104] Mark 14:15.

Christ and the descent of the Holy Spirit at Pentecost this room is called by another Greek name (*huperoion*),[105] which, however, has the same meaning.

It is the upper portion of the house, used by the family for any great occasion, but always especially set apart for guests — the "best" room. Usually one gains access to it from the outside, in order to avoid the necessity of passing through the service rooms and the bedrooms on the ground floor, and it is often preceded by a terrace with wide bays, unless it opens onto a courtyard.

The upper room of the paschal supper was a particularly large one, which is a further argument in favor of its identification with the room of Pentecost, in which Peter was able to address a crowd of 120 persons. It was furnished and ready, that is, provided with carpet, cushions, and tables.

In giving His disciples such accurate instructions as to what they are to ask for, Jesus knows what the response will be. He knows the good will of the man in question and He counts upon it. In any case, during the feast it is understood at Jerusalem that any apartment not occupied or to let is to be regarded as common property; the firstcomer may, without indiscretion, demand the use of it. The visitor must, of course, supply his own provisions, and Jesus makes a point of doing this, not only out of thoughtfulness, but also probably in order to ensure that the privacy which He desires shall not be disturbed by the presence of any strangers.

In the early days the Jew had to eat the Passover standing, his loins girt, a staff in his hand, sandals on his feet; and he had to eat

---

[105] Acts 1:13.

hurriedly, to signify the hasty departure from Egypt. But at the time of Christ it is no longer so. The rabbinical interpreters prescribe the ordinary posture, and the participants signify their freedom by adopting the reclining position, which is the right of masters. Even slaves, to whom this posture is normally forbidden, are allowed to assume it on this day, as a sign of the freedom of the people of Israel.

The guests, therefore, eat the paschal lamb lying on mattresses or carpets laid upon the ground, with the left elbow on a cushion and the right arm free. The food is set on one or more large dishes on a low table, so that each can easily reach it. The food is not passed around among the guests; each helps himself or dips his bread into the dish as he requires it. "He that dippeth his hand with me in the dish . . . ," says Jesus later to His disciples.[106] Strictly speaking, one might suppose that couches and higher tables were used, as with the *triclinium*,[107] but these were not yet in general use in the East.

∞

Apparently Jesus did not consider that His intention to institute a new rite upon that day dispensed Him from celebrating the Jewish Passover. It was of the Jewish Passover that the disciples spoke, and Jesus did not correct them; and all the preparations, preparations mentioned by Christ Himself in the instructions given to His disciples, have reference to the Jewish feast. He has no intention of omitting the Passover, nor yet does He make it an empty show. He embodies it in His own designs and thus shows its

[106] Mark 14:20.

[107] A Latin term referring to a couch running around three sides of a table for reclining on at meals.

true prophetic meaning. The ceremony which He has in mind is like Jerusalem's Gate of Ephraim: the entrance and the exit are in different directions: the faithful enter as Jews and come out as Christians.

∞

Jesus reclines in the place of honor, as befits the rabbi. The Twelve — Judas included — are ranged around the table at each side of Him. John is in the second place of honor, close by His Master's right, able by a simple movement to lay his head upon the sacred breast. Peter is next to John, to whom he can whisper in secret. Judas is not far from his Master, for he, too, is able to receive a warning from Jesus intended for his ear alone. Could it be that Judas is on the Master's left, in the first place of honor among the disciples? . . .

Jesus speaks, and His first words are these: "With desire have I desired to eat this Passover with you, before I suffer."[108] These words are a sigh of love from His heart as He begins this banquet from which He awaits such great results. They are the preliminary chord of a harpist's melody. The heart of the Master is filled with vibrations, and it needs only the shock of a new event to awaken it to music of tenderness.

Normally, the burden of His discourse was too serious to allow Jesus to give full vent to the love that filled His heart. He felt it necessary sometimes even to react violently against the natural bent of His affections: "Woman, what is it to me and to thee?"[109] "Who are my mother and my brethren?"[110] "Suffer the dead to bury

[108]Luke 22:15.
[109]John 2:4.
[110]Matt. 12:48; Mark 3:33.

their dead."[111] "Get behind me, Satan, thou art a scandal unto me."[112] But this divine harshness is only proof of a complete devotion to His high purpose, and His tenderness shows itself at the first opportunity.

Now He is about to die and the imminence of the end, the thought that soon He must leave those whom He loves, calls forth the unrestrained outpourings of His loving heart.

"With desire have I desired to eat this Passover with you." For Him it is the last Passover; and for His people, too, it is the last Passover that will be legitimate. Tomorrow Judaism will be a glance backwards; today it is still a prophecy.

Jesus has ardently desired to eat this Passover, this last Passover which is on the brink of the kingdom of Heaven, the Passover of the new era in which the Crucified will reign. This night and the morrow are to be marked by functions of gloom and sorrow; but they will open with a Mass of joy.

But what a mixed joy is this! Who but a divine artist can bring into a supreme harmony sentiments so conflicting and so diverse! In St. Luke the dominant note is one of fulfilled desire; but the three other evangelists set sorrow in the foreground. Treason is in their midst, the shadow of the Cross darkens the supper table. How can they rejoice? And yet how can they not rejoice when love is giving its all!

Jesus feels that He has already passed the portals of death, and He is about to institute the memorial of His passing: "Now I am not in the world."[113] He feels that He is already living His unending life, and He distributes its fruits to the human race. He is full of joy in His death.

[111] Matt. 8:22; Luke 9:60.
[112] Matt. 16:23.
[113] John 17:11.

∞

The paschal supper might begin at any moment after the appearance of the first three stars; often it began a little later. It is therefore already dark, and the time on that account more propitious for intimate revelations. They will have chosen a lamb, one year old, without spot or blemish. It will have been offered on the altar in the Temple, and it will have been cooked and served in accordance with the rites of which we still find traces in the *Mishnah*.[114]

While the lamb was being eaten, the head of the family had to explain solemnly, in answer to the question of the youngest child, the symbolic meaning of the food set before them. The lamb commemorated the redemption and the salvation of Israel when the angel was bringing death to every dwelling. The mixture of cooked fruits, in its reddish sauce, signified the mortar of Pithom and Rameses during the days of hard labor in Egypt. The bitter herbs recalled the anguish of those days, while the *azyme*, or unleavened bread, signified the haste with which their ancestors had fled from the land.

Jesus can invest this teaching with a new significance. He indeed knows who is the Lamb of the true Passover, from what slavery and anguish He is going to deliver us, and what this swift journey is upon which the new Israelites are to embark. They are to pass from evil to good, from spiritual slavery to the freedom of sons, from the kingdom of Satan to the kingdom of God on earth, and from this earth to Heaven. This will be the burden of His speech during the evening.

[114]The first part of the *Talmud*, the authoritative compilation of oral traditions regarding the application of Jewish law, which is still in use today.

After the explanation of the rite, a part of the *Hallel*, or "Song of Praise," was sung. This was a selection from Psalms 112 to 117,[115] the most vivid passages concerning the Messiah and His sufferings, those which most clearly indicated His redemptive work and its prefigurations in the history of the Jews. The cup was passed around four times. During the intervals the food was eaten, according to rites which varied from Hillel to Schammai.[116] The last part of the *Hallel*, a hymn of triumphant thanksgiving to Yahweh, was sung before the fourth cup.

All this was doubtless observed exactly; but the purpose of this final assembly was quite different in reality. The accounts given in the Gospels seem to hurry over the description of the Jewish Passover; indeed, only St. Luke distinguishes clearly between the two stages in the repast. The others mention the Jewish Passover only in connection with the preparations; when they come to the actual meal, they pass quickly over that which was destined to perish, to tell us more directly of that which was to endure.

Jesus, who left to two delegates the task of preparing for the Jewish repast, proceeds now to make His own preparations; and here it is not a matter of house, table, cushions, or provisions. He has to prepare the heart. Wishing to leave a great example of what He has always presented as the sum total of His teaching, and to interpret beforehand His spiritual banquet in the sense of that unity which He has come to establish, He rises from the table. He takes off His cloak and girds His loins with a cloth. Taking the vessel of water with the basin provided for the ablutions, He kneels on two knees before each of those present, and begins to wash their feet.

[115]RSV = Pss. 113-118.

[116]Important Jewish rabbis, or teachers of Jewish law, who were active from roughly 50 B.C. to A.D. 30.

Imagine the astonishment of the Twelve at this spectacle! St. John describes the scene in solemn terms upon which Simon Peter's protest is a sort of commentary: "Lord, dost Thou wash my feet? . . . Thou shalt never wash my feet!" But Jesus, "knowing that the Father has given Him all things into His hands, and that He came from God and goeth to God," will not be deterred from His task.[117] The evangelist's account invests the act with a religious and eternal significance.

The symbol of love is mingled with the symbol of purity, so that we may learn that where true love is, there also is the assembly of the saints. Jesus does not need to be purified, but He humbles Himself and He loves. He gives an example of every virtue. By this act He affirms that the enemy of love is pride, and that the enemy of all good is the refusal to love. Humility and charity are the foundation and the crown respectively of the spiritual edifice which He intends to erect, both in the individual and in the human race. And the Cross, too, which supports this edifice, is as humiliating as it is painful; but when the work is accomplished it will be glorious as the instrument of union and the source of bliss. Everything is there. All is in the Cross, because all is in humility and love, and the washing of the feet is the herald of the Cross.

How they need to be cleansed, these poor feet with which we touch the earth! Even though the head that thinks, the heart that loves, the hands that act may pursue ends which are pure, yet our feet trail in the dust and are soiled by the mud from the road they tread. We need the pitcher of water and the touch of the Savior's hands. We need submission to cleansing grace if, with Peter protesting and yet converted, we will "have part" in the gift Jesus brings: "If I wash thee not, thou shalt have no part with me."[118]

[117]John 13:3-10.
[118]John 13:8.

A moment later Jesus shows that the washing of the feet has still another meaning. He speaks of His Apostles, and of the unity that He has come to establish between them and Him, a unity like that between Him and His Father. Jesus washes the feet of the Twelve to prepare them for their journeys across the earth. Purity and humility are the condition of love; and love is the soul of the apostolate. The world will be conquered by those whom Jesus has convinced that this is the proper order of things, by those whom He has animated with this manifold power.

One might say that He, the divine Apostle, kneels in admiration before these other Apostles whom He is soon to send to the ends of the earth, and who are soon to devote themselves so generously and so effectively to their work: "How beautiful upon the mountains are the feet of him that bringeth good tidings, and that preacheth peace: of him that sheweth forth good!"[119] The prophet had Christ especially in mind; but what Christ has received He communicates to His own, and there He kneels in humility before the gift from on high.

Resuming His cloak and taking His place once more at the table, Jesus now explains the act which He has performed, and His words are full of exalted teaching. During the whole of this night He pours out His heart in expressions of love, with warnings, too, and sometimes with tender reproaches. Jesus gives to His disciples a complete spiritual testament, especially a testament of love — "a flood of love," as St. Anselm calls it — and at the same time a torrent of sublimity.

Read once again this discourse related by St. John and see how full it is of wondrous sayings. Jesus comforts the Eleven on the eve of the tribulations of which Judas' departure gives the signal, for

[119] Isa. 52:7.

them as well as for Himself. He warns them of their weakness and bids them to be of good heart. He foretells their abandonment of Him, adding with tender solicitude, "Let not your heart be troubled; you believe in God, believe also in me."[120] He tells them of the mansions that are in the house of His Father, so that to them they may direct their steps.[121] He is going to "prepare a place" for them,[122] and "it is expedient for them" that He should go,[123] so that the Spirit who enlightens, guides, and consoles may come upon them. He "will not leave them orphans";[124] they know already that under a twofold mysterious form He will come to them. He leaves them His peace, He gives them His peace, but not as the world gives, for the world gives only a false peace. And so that this peace may dwell in all, He renews the commandment of mutual love, which He sets before them as the sign and the measure of the love that men will have for Him.

"A new commandment I give unto you; that you love one another as I have loved you, that you also love one another. By this shall all men know that you are my disciples, if you have love one for another."[125] He insists upon the commandment of love in the very moment in which He is about to give that great proof of love, of which He says, "Greater love than this no man hath, that he lay down his life for his friends."[126]

And now in the midst of this discourse, which together with the washing of the feet has aroused the emotions of the Twelve to

[120]John 14:1.
[121]John 14:2.
[122]John 14:2-3.
[123]John 16:7.
[124]John 14:18.
[125]John 13:34-35.
[126]John 15:13.

a high pitch of emotion, comes a stage in the repast which drives home these teachings and gives the symbols their full meaning. It is the moment of the institution of the Eucharist.

∞

After He had said, "With desire have I desired to eat this Passover with you," Jesus had added, "For I say to you that from this time I will not eat it, till it be fulfilled in the kingdom of God."[127] The Jewish Passover, which Jesus is celebrating in this very moment, is to be fulfilled, like the rest of the Law of which He had said, "I am not come to destroy but to fulfill."[128]

And in what kingdom of God will this fulfillment take place? Certainly outside this world, in the place in which Jesus is now going and to which His disciples will one day follow Him. But this fulfillment will also take place — such seems to be the meaning of St. Luke's words — in the kingdom of God which He is establishing upon earth, in that kingdom for which He is legislating during these last discourses.

There are thus two stages: the Jewish Passover is transformed into the Eucharistic Passover; the Eucharistic Passover will one day be transformed into the heavenly Passover. And for Jesus, who also takes communion at the Last Supper, this last transformation is just about to take place.

To the disciples, those who lived in the Holy Land and those of all ages, the new repast will appear in the light of a memorial. Jesus contrives to render it a memorial more touching and consoling than any figure could be, for to the commemoration which recalls the past He adds the efficacy of His own real presence.

[127] Luke 22:15-16.
[128] Matt. 5:17.

Before He departs He fills the void which His departure will leave. He gives comfort to the future, assuring us that He will not leave us orphans. He perpetuates His passing amongst those who survive. He is about to found His everlasting dwelling place, and in a humble commemorative repast the whole reality of the divine Gift will be the treasure of souls.

Jesus, then, "taking bread, gave thanks and brake; and gave to them, saying: This is my body, which is given for you. Do this for a commemoration of me. In like manner the chalice also, after He had supped, saying: This is the chalice, the new testament in my blood, which shall be shed for you."[129]

Two things are here combined, and the one presupposes the other. There is a spiritual food, which Jesus Himself provides, and there is a perpetual sacrifice, which is the very sacrifice of Jesus Himself, and which obtains for us its fruits.

"The little ones have asked for bread, and there was none to break it unto them."[130] There had been the manna; in the Temple there were always the loaves of proposition; at Cana and on the banks of the lake Jesus Himself had given a miraculous food. But none of this was the true bread. The true bread had to be steeped in blood, broken with the gesture of loving sacrifice, distributed in the communion of a banquet for the whole world, and this upon a hill which foreshadowed Calvary, and like Calvary was destined to endure forever.

Jesus takes the bread and "gives thanks." This was His way of blessing; but in both cases, here and in the multiplication of the loaves, His formula of blessing is announced in solemn form. This blessing is repeated over the chalice, and when St. Paul speaks of this he emphasizes the obvious reason for this special blessing: it is

[129]Luke 22:19-20.
[130]Lam. 4:4.

because the chalice of the Supper is truly and strictly a blessed cup, but only when it is blessed with due solemnity. "The chalice of benediction which we bless," says the Apostle.[131]

There must have been something characteristic in the gesture with which Jesus distributed this food to them, because they are able to recognize Him by this alone. Little children are familiar with the gesture with which their mother gives them bread to eat. We have only to add to this loving tenderness a divine majesty in order to visualize the action of Jesus Himself.

But still more in a moral sense it is true that Jesus is recognized in the breaking of bread. He alone gives the bread that nourishes and strengthens, the bread of sweetness and hope that produces everlasting life. Since the Last Supper the hand of Jesus has been stretched forth to us all so that we may recognize Him thus. His bread is multiplied according to our number, our needs, and our desires. His chalice is one, as a sign of our unity, but it makes its way throughout the whole earth and the whole of time, as in the Cenacle it went around the table. On that day Jesus truly prepared food for all ages. In His kingdom none can starve unless he wills it. Forever, as at Emmaus, as on the banks of the lake when the risen Christ appears in the whiteness of the morning, in Heaven itself, Jesus may be recognized in the breaking of bread.

The bread of the Jewish Passover had to be broken into little pieces, to signify sacrifice. Jesus apparently contented Himself with dividing it into portions. But clearly the breaking of the bread has for Him also the symbolism of sacrifice, His own sacrifice, since He refers to the bread thus broken as His body which is "given" or "delivered up,"[132] and because this gift is in fact a gift unto death.

[131] 1 Cor. 10:16.
[132] Luke 18:32, 22:19.

The wine that flows like blood, the wine that *is* blood, is given in the same manner. Jesus drinks of it also, as a sign of perfect union; He tastes of His own sacrifice. I see Him on the Cross joyously shedding every drop from His veins. May we not think of Him as represented in the ancient pictures, filling the chalice that the Church presents to Him, or pouring forth the torrent of life, that all men may drink of it?

In the Greek rite, the celebrant pierces the sacred species with a small lance as he says these words from the Gospel: "One of the soldiers pierced His side with a lance."[133] When Jesus, still alive on the Cross, saw the lance of Longinus[134] passing to and fro before Him, must He not have thought of that generous cup into which He was to pour His last drops of blood, as a sign of boundless love?

On Calvary Jesus loves even beyond the limits of death; in the Cenacle He anticipates its hour. On the Cross He consummates His visible and bloody sacrifice; in the sacrament He conceals the sacrifice, and even Himself. But in both cases death is the source of life. It is because He is to die that He first institutes a memorial of His death; but it is because He has died that this memorial is the mightiest and the sweetest of all life-giving things.

"Do this in commemoration of me," He says. The Apostles are thus ordained priests and the faithful made perpetual partakers of the altar. The host will be raised up as Christ was lifted up on the Cross; it will be broken as He was broken under the blows of His tormentors; it will be given to the innocent Christian as His body was committed to the new tomb.

O Jesus, hanging on the Cross, with what gentle love must You regard this house of mysteries! How brightly that little house of

---

[133] John 19:34.

[134] The name traditionally given to the soldier who pierced the side of Christ with his spear.

Zion shines out from the gloom that covers Moriah and its ancient glory! From that house flows a stream of life; tomorrow it will be a stream of light. And the moment is at hand when Cenacle, Temple, and Cross will be but one, when the house of Your Father will be Your house, will be the ho   giving sacrifice and of Your resplendent glory, and   per room" for Your table and for Your Spirit.

Then the Cenacle of Mount Zio   r preserve its ancient traces. The Cenacle will b   Ve ourselves, Your children, shall be a cenacle in   ing of bread will be spiritually renewed; where the   that breaking will be accepted in the spirit of sa   ur food will be assimilated, Your Spirit manifested   ope, in the glory of good works.

Say now when You will, "*Consumn*   all is now ready for the consummation of justice a

∞

The past and the future are as distinct for Jesus as they are distinct in themselves. He sees them as different and distant from each other, but their distance is in a manner spatial, such as not to prevent their being present together before His gaze. As God sees the procession of time from the heights of eternity as from an immovable peak, so His Christ, associated with Him in eternity, sees as God and knows as man what the future of His work has in store. Thus as He looks toward the holy Mount of Zion He can see in one perspective the sacred repast of yesterday together with the graces which are reserved for tomorrow.

[135]"It is consummated"; John 19:30.

Already before the Cross Jesus was dead in spirit; in spirit He had risen already before the tomb. With His all-seeing glance, Jesus visits now the scenes of His posthumous appearances and of Pentecost, as He had doubtless many a time visited Calvary while He walked around the city of Jerusalem. What a thrill must have passed through the Son of Man when in the full vigor of life He came forth from the Gate of Ephraim and trod the path of Golgotha with its flowers of ruddy hue! He could mark the very place of the Cross, for was it not preordained from all eternity?

And now as He gazes at the Cenacle it is to the future that He looks, and His heart swells with hope as He foresees the works of the Spirit. He is racked by pain that seems almost to overwhelm Him; but He finds comfort in memory, and anticipation fills Him with joy.

The outpourings of the Last Supper are only an omen of the apparently greater and public outpourings which will later on win the world for His work. His glance lingers and He prophesies. The Cross is the link between two eras, whose harmony is for us an eternal object of contemplation.

Immediately after the death of their Master the terrified disciples will recover from their panic; they will gather to talk concerning Him and to devote themselves to prayer. The disciples of Emmaus, when they return to Jerusalem, will find once more assembled "the Eleven and those that were with them."[136] The women who have been to the empty tomb similarly repair to a group consisting of the Eleven and all the rest (that is, those who

[136]Luke 24:33.

were closely connected with the Apostles and together with them form Mary's entourage).

There is no mystery as to the place where they are assembled. We are told the place to which the Eleven betook themselves when they returned to the city after witnessing the Ascension: "And when they were come in, they went up into an upper room where [the Apostles] abode."[137] They are therefore in the Cenacle, "with the women and Mary, the mother of Jesus, and His brethren" (that is, His cousins).[138]

And now this house, which was the scene of the farewell on the evening of Holy Thursday, which has welcomed the remnant of the group when the tomb seems to have ended all, is to witness their reunion and to be the scene of the confirmation of the disciples' faltering faith.

Meanwhile Jesus on the Cross is so far from resenting the frailty of these poor human beings, that He is actually planning the means for overcoming it. He will show Himself living to those who do not believe in His survival, glorious to those who think Him defeated, always loving toward those who might well expect reproach. But reproach them He will; now, upon the very eve of their mission, is not the time to overlook their infirmity. Nevertheless, He will calm their fears beforehand with His customary salutation: "Peace be with you; it is I, fear not."[139] Then, seeing that their terror remains and their doubts endure — for the apparition coming upon them so suddenly, "the doors being shut,"[140] seems to be a "spirit"[141] — He will speak thus gently to them:

[137] Acts 1:13.
[138] Acts 1:14.
[139] Luke 24:36.
[140] John 20:19.
[141] Luke 24:37.

"Why are you troubled, and why do thoughts arise in your hearts? See my hands and feet, that it is I myself; touch and see: for a spirit hath not flesh and bones, as you see me to have."[142]

Still they will hesitate, this time from a joyous surprise to which they fear to yield lest they be disappointed. Then Jesus will ask them for something to eat; they will offer Him some dry fish and honey. He will take it and share it with them, as though the everlasting banquet which He had foretold at the Supper were already taking place, and they were His guests.

Moreover, He will allow one of their number to be absent from this meeting — a divine ruse to aid their faith. Thomas, doubting Thomas, enthusiastic but somewhat strongheaded, will be skeptical of the news brought by his brethren: "Except I shall see in His hands the print of the nails, and put my finger into the place of the nails, and put my hand into His side, I will not believe."[143]

Thomas is the type of the unreasonable man, of the man who is not satisfied to receive information by the ordinary channels, who rejects the law of solidarity — which rules the dissemination of knowledge like everything else — and requires special evidence for himself. He wants a providential arrangement for his own particular benefit. Jesus blames Thomas; but He yields, and when finally He has proven His own love, the disciple gives vent to his: "My Lord and my God!"[144]

∽

From that moment, and as a first consequence of the Supper, the Cenacle is destined to change its character. From being a

[142] Luke 24:39.
[143] John 20:25.
[144] John 20:28.

reception room or dining hall, it becomes a place of prayer and religious expectancy, a temporary chapel, pending the time when the new Church will take its place and consecrate a solemn cult to the Conqueror of death.

Mary, the holy women, and the disciples go there to honor the sacred memory and the mystic presence. This place is a sacred place. And as Jesus gazes upon it from the Cross He hallows it once more, consecrating as a perpetual sanctuary this room so blessed, the house of the new Bread and the abode of the Spirit.

∞

Jesus had said, "If I go not, the Paraclete will not come to you."[145] The Cross has merited this divine guest for us. No sooner has the price been paid, no sooner have souls been prepared to receive Him, than He comes, this Paraclete, to fulfill His solemn and everlasting mission. He is accompanied by manifest signs: a mighty wind that shakes the whole house, a fire that divides into flaming tongues to rest upon each of those present, an influence that shows itself in speech of diverse tongues — symbols of the mission of the disciples and of the work of the Church. But if He shows Himself externally, it is especially within that He acts; for the Paraclete is recognized above all things in the stirring of the human heart.

The divine Spirit is a Spirit of holiness. It is He who creates the *Holy* Church. He does not make it free from every stain, or make its members — or even its heads — impeccable, but sets within it a source of sanctity. Just as a river runs swiftly at the middle and sleeps sluggishly at its banks or in its backwaters, so is it with the

[145]John 16:7.

69

stream of sanctity in the Church; and each of us, with the aid of God, may choose the pace that he wills. The essential thing is to reach these waters.

Come, ye men, sinners in Adam, by yourselves always exposed to danger of sin, guilty always to some degree, piteously weak — come! Regeneration awaits you here, and with it strength and protection.

∞

The divine Spirit is a Spirit of organization. Before He can create the *Holy* Church He must first create the Church. He must become the soul of this body, stimulate its functions, establish a subordination of parts, and send coursing throughout a unifying principle of government, which the theologians call *Orders.* The election of Matthias in the Cenacle serves as the first sign of this role of the Paraclete, and the hierarchy is its perpetual manifestation. Holy Orders is a social grace, a collective gift of God, from which a host of others proceeds.

∞

The divine Spirit is also a witness. "He will bear testimony of me," the Master had said.[146] And how mighty is the testimony that the Spirit of Jesus bears! He bears testimony by word, by martyrdom, by genius, and by virtue. He bears testimony by the life of individuals and by the life of peoples. He adds to that testimony the miracles which in every age spring up in the path that the Spirit follows. He bears testimony, too, by the very texture of what

---

[146]John 15:26.

He offers, by the inner harmony which He manifests to us, and I know of no mightier testimony than this.

Life bears testimony to life, being to being. That which is self-contained and consistent bears the mark of God. Now the Spirit of Christ is a full life, a harmony without a false note, a logic that never falters; and its simplicity reveals creative art.

See the divine simplicity of the Gospel and of the catechism, the simplicity of the soul of Christ and of the souls of the saints! This ineffable simplicity contains superhuman wisdom, and the pure and limpid style in which that wisdom loves to flow, like clear water in crystal, reveals all its wondrous depths.

Those who understand this find in it an irresistible attraction. Mystery cramps the spirit; but the convergence and the coherence of mysteries are a beam of light that illuminates the whole. We feel that here is truth, because here is unity, with which truth is one. From this arises certitude, which makes mystery a bliss.

There is no man-made doctrine that unifies and reconciles all the manifestations of life. Only once has the seamless coat been seen. It is here. The Spirit shows it to us, with its tissue of rays issuing in a single light.

The word of the Spirit is as clear as the voice of the ocean at night. It is at night that the giant sea drowns the mutterings of its single waves in one mighty voice. And so it is with the Spirit. The Spirit is the one explanation, as He will be the one power, as He will be the one everlasting joy, for He is happy and radiant peace.

∞

Furthermore (and indeed, as a consequence of this), the divine Spirit will be a Spirit of victory. He will breathe to the ends of the earth, shaking the universe as He shook the little house that was built upon the hill. It is through Him that the Man who was lifted up from the earth will draw all things to Himself. The Spirit will be like a consuming fire, a fire whose light shines from afar, a fire that rages on, setting forests and mountains ablaze. "I am come to cast fire upon the earth," said Jesus, "and what will I, but that it be kindled?"[147] To fulfill the desire of His zeal, Jesus has only to cast this brand abroad.

His work will not be like that of any man of genius, whose posterity is always restricted. What son of men would have dared to say "Go ye, and teach all nations"?[148] Would not the very next generation have given the lie to so daring a claim?

The greatest names of history have lived only in men's memory. The living progeny of heroes has always been small, transitory, and usually unfaithful. They had not the power, as Jesus had, of communicating to that progeny a living Spirit.

Aristotle, Alexander, Michelangelo, and St. Louis saw their work ruined by successors or poor imitators, or by so-called disciples whose real aim was to acquire reputation for themselves on the strength of a heritage received. Jesus saves His work and makes it live, because He dwells in it forever. He possesses the means of preserving its initial inspiration. He can give it perennial youth; He can make it that fountain of water springing up into life everlasting, of which He spoke to the Samaritan woman. And He does this by His Spirit.

Thanks to the Holy Spirit, the universal Church is always the Church, despite the diversity of local and superficial tendencies. The Church realizes the ideal of the "permanence of the type" which may always vary in living species. The essential guiding principle is immutable, and it remains so while the Church advances on all fronts, like an army using every weapon but led by a

[147]Luke 12:49.
[148]Matt. 28:19.

single plan. The dogma of the Church, Her ethical doctrine, Her discipline, Her sacramental Liturgy, Her hierarchical constitution are essentially today what they were in the time of St. Paul — what they are in the Cenacle.

There have been individual defections, many of them. There have been collective maladies. Yet it has always been a living Church that was sick, or else one or other member or function, and the Church has not on that account been reduced to the state of a corpse. Its infirmity, like that of Lazarus, was "not unto death."[149] The Church does not die. The Church throbs with life, and the times of defection are precisely those which stimulate the Spirit to violent and wonderful reactions.

Troubled times are times of sanctity and heroism. In every socially disinherited epoch it seems that there are powerful personalities destined to concentrate and hold in reserve the spiritual activity of the community. They are the leaven of the future. And this is the work of the Spirit, an interior flame, a living flame not unlike that which gives life to our bodies and animates our homes and our cities.

∞

Finally, when we have said that the divine Spirit conquers and organizes, it would seem unnecessary to say that He unifies. But we must remark the universal character of this unity.

The Spirit transcends all differences in creation; He is the Spirit of spirits, the Spirit of all beings. All things depend upon Him, and when He stirs we must expect a universal movement. Until Pentecost the world was a chaos, or to the extent that it was

[149] John 11:4.

organized, as in the Synagogue, it was in virtue of the anticipated action of the Spirit. The influence of the Cenacle reached back into the ages of the past.

But it is in the Spirit's influence on the future that His greatest power is manifest. The Spirit polarizes the world; He polarizes the ages. He gathers "into one the children of God, that were dispersed";[150] and those who think to escape Him fulfill His purpose in another way and serve the interests of the elect.

The world was without life, a corpse, a Lazarus in its winding bands, stinking of corruption — for its elements and its powers were dissipated. The Spirit of Christ restores the unifying principles of life, and the universe stands erect and alive once more.

This unity is manifested in the language of Christianity, which presents the doctrine that codifies the whole of life as one and identical in all ages and in every land. For all the diversity of accent that we may find here or there, yesterday or today, the language of Christianity is one voice across the ages, in every civilization and in every people. There will be many witnesses, but only one testimony. The gift of tongues, which has been granted to Christian doctrine as it was granted to its first preachers, is the gift of making men hear in different spiritual idioms a language which is one, of expanding the white light of Heaven in the prism of human understanding.

It is due to the Spirit that the message of Jesus gives expression to another world, and that this other world and the world of pilgrimage are but one. The kingdom of God is everywhere, and the Spirit is its light. And as there is one light, so there is one orientation, one action, and one issue, which is — invisibly here and clearly hereafter — everlasting life.

[150]John 11:52.

The divine Spirit is a Spirit of eternity. The living water that Jesus gives must return to its own level. It came from Heaven, and back to Heaven it springs, to abide there eternally. Heaven is its surface of equilibrium, and if "Christ having risen, dieth now no more,"[151] "if where He is, He wills and grants that we also may be,"[152] the reason is that His Spirit breathes between the Father and the Word. And it is in the Word Incarnate and by Him that we receive the divine life of grace.

∞

The Cross is now streaming with blood. The Savior groans in pain, but the groaning Savior is like the laborer who pants as he works at his task. When the task is completed it will appear that means and end are proportionate to each other, and that the Eternal Witness did not lie.

[151] Rom. 6:9.
[152] Cf. John 14:3.

5

The Mount of Olives

The Mount of Olives assumes in the vision of Jesus an importance proportionate to that which it held in His Passion and in His public life in Judea. It is the pediment of the natural frame which surrounds the Cross; and after being the theater of the great conflict it is to be the point of departure for a glorious mission.

Gethsemane is at the foot of the hill, on a lower level than Calvary. Jesus cannot see it; the porch of Solomon hides it from sight, as a mountain wall hides a gulf.

The Mount of Olives is called by this name in the Gospels. Josephus[153] calls it "the Mount of the Olive yard" or simply "the Olive yard." It is often called Mount Olivet, after the Latin *olivetum* ("olive grove"). The brow of this mountain bounds the horizon of Jerusalem to the east, and it can be seen from any part of the city. For those who live in Jerusalem it holds an irresistible attraction, for even apart from its eminence and its importance, at

[153] Jewish historian (c. A.D. 37-100) whose book, *The Jewish War*, is a key source for the history of the Holy Land in the years A.D. 66-70.

77

no point in the landscape can one enjoy to greater advantage the symbolical beauty of the symphony of light: in the late autumn, as early as four o'clock in the morning, dawn extends above this mountain its veil of blue, green, pink, and gold. It is alive, but with the calm beauty of a happy death, while above, through the filmy tiers of cloud, a bright jewel shines out, a shimmering flame like an archangel's lance, with a light of incomparable softness. It is the morning star, which Jesus made a symbol of Himself.

We read the following lines in the book of Revelation: "I am the root and stock of David, the bright and morning star";[154] and elsewhere: "He that shall overcome and keep my works unto the end. . . . I will give him the morning star."[155] The Christian who has lived in the Holy Land sees the meaning of this promise. He understands why this bright star is associated with the mortal apotheosis of his Savior. On this very morning, the fourteenth Nisan,[156] Jesus saw this pure symbol appear before the coming of the sun. He saw it vanish gracefully, as He Himself was soon to yield Himself trustfully into the arms of His Father.

In the evening the Mount of Olives receives only the reflection of the sunset, but this is its most beautiful part. It is a sunset that seems a dawn, for it has all its calm and peaceful beauty. The crest of the mountain stands out pale against the moving shades of violet traversed by green and gold. Deep grey wisps of cloud hang themselves lightly upon it, only to disappear into the still transparent shadow beyond. The night falls imperceptibly, but ever luminous, and when the moon is full, none can describe the

[154]Rev. 22:16.

[155]Rev. 2:26-28.

[156]Nisan is the first month in the Jewish year, roughly equivalent to April. The Passover lamb was traditionally sacrificed on the fourteenth day of Nisan.

virginal majesty of that silvery orb as it rests upon its ground of glimmering mauve.

The Mount of Olives is truly for Jerusalem the region of light. And we love it because it shone for Jesus and cast a halo over His days. As He came forth from the Temple by the Golden Gate, Jesus had it before Him. As He came from Bethany in the morning He saw its clear outline glowing red, until it served as an eminence from which He might view the glittering domes of the city.

This road between Jerusalem and Bethany leads on to Jericho; it cuts the mountain in almost equal parts. Leading to the Jordan is another road, further to the south and not so steep, and there is a third road which bears to the north. It is the middle road that attracts our chief attention, because Jesus must have passed along it many times during His public life. David, His ancestor, had climbed this slope as he fled from Absalom, suffering without revenge the insults of Shimei who cast stones and dust at him as he passed.[157] The example of the pardon of the Cross went far back into history.

This rising path is the last that Jesus trod upon earth. It is the road taken by the Good Samaritan, whose symbolism is embodied in Him. It was on this roadside that the two blind men — brethren of ours — were healed.[158] And it was at the end of this road, in Jericho itself, that another of our brethren, Zacchaeus the publican, came down joyously from his sycamore tree to lead pardon and peace into his sinful house.[159]

At the eastern foot of the mountain the three roads enter a dreary looking region: the desert of Judea, seamed and slashed with valleys in every direction, like waves congealed in their rising.

---

[157] 2 Kings 16:13 (RSV = 2 Sam. 16:13).
[158] Matt. 9:27-30.
[159] Luke 19:1-10.

Here the solitude is as solemn and harsh as the words of the prophets, harsh as the words of Amos the shepherd and prophet who hurled his anathemas upon Tekoa, which is part of this desolate land.

It is from here that comes the burning wind which parches the land of Judea, as the breath of evil sterilizes the soul. The ancient Jews saw in this desert the region of sin. The neighborhood of the Dead Sea evoked in their minds the thought of God's avenging visitations, and this is the reason why every year they drove into this desert the scapegoat, laden with the sins of Israel. The beast was solemnly cursed before the altar, driven into the valley of Kedron, where it was cast down into the deep abyss as a sacrifice for the people.

Jesus, as He looks in this direction from the Cross, cannot fail to reflect that He is this beast accursed, driven this very day out of the city, shut out from the world, driven forth to die, humbly and silently allowing Himself to be counted among the goats.

In this bleak and arid region, on this earth clothed in nothing save its silence, its burning light, and its wind, John the Baptist lived and played his part as herald of the Messiah. In the desert he opened the future way of peoples. He obeyed the ancient prophet: "Prepare ye the way of the Lord, make straight in the wilderness the paths of our God."[160]

Dressed in camel's hair, the material with which the Bedouins make their tents, eating roasted locusts and wild honey, John passed through the land strangely exalted, moved by a mighty spirit. In him the New Testament sought itself in the Old, the Old strove after its metamorphosis. The past was filled with a great expectation and thrilled with what the future might bring.

[160] Isa. 40:3.

John was the voice of the desert crying after refreshing waters, the voice from afar calling to Him "that was to come,"[161] the voice of narrow-minded righteousness and legal virtue calling for the opening of the soul and for purifying penance to greet the coming of love. Such was John the Baptist, and his voice filled Judea as the voice of Jesus was soon to fill the world.

And let us not forget that Jesus willed to associate Himself with this period of preparation, and in a manner to be a precursor to Himself. For forty days at the beginning of His public life He dwelt in the desert, giving Himself up to prayer and fasting, setting His divine plans in order, arranging the future, accepting and adapting His task, and choosing out those who would assist Him — and with no other witness save nature for this inauguration of the kingdom.

It was not far from the Jordan that He abode, in the district now known as that of the "Forty Days," among the jackals and small panthers such as are still to be found there today. His companions — for the first time, it would seem, since He had reached the age of manhood — were those invisible beings, those legions of His Father who were to accompany Him wherever He went. Jesus could brave the solitude, for He bore His universe within Himself.

Nearer at hand, and within the walls of the city, the dying glance of Jesus divines another spot of great symbolical importance, to which He had given His consecration. I mean the pool of Siloam,[162] where the man born blind received his miraculous cure. The man born blind is man himself, who is blind by nature, and Siloam is the Messiah, "He that is sent," who begins here His cleansing mission by water, later to achieve it by blood.

[161] Matt. 3:11; Mark 1:7; Luke 3:16.
[162] John 9.

On the same line of vision, but far distant, is Machaerus, where the Precursor was slain, and Mount Nebo, which buried Moses with his hope.

∞

Coming back to the Mount of Olives we must also mention Bethphage, on its lower eastern slopes. Jesus cannot see it, but it was here that only yesterday He commanded the ass to be loosed and preparations to be made for that fleeting triumph, that triumph which was mingled with His tears over the city, a triumph that was decisive only in the sense that it decided His death. This triumph was closely connected with that which He had won at the tomb of Lazarus, and it was precisely in freeing Lazarus from his bands that He had opened His own tomb.

Visitors are still shown the *Lazarion*, or Tomb of Lazarus, near Bethany, now known as *El-Azarieh* — the town of Lazarus. It has undergone various changes, but it is still quite impressive and vividly recalls the miracle. There you can see the cave from which the man who had dwelt in the great night haggardly emerged. The groove of the stone still remains. The spot in which Jesus stood can hardly have changed, and it is equally clear where the two sisters were. You may see the scene as Rembrandt saw it in his great watercolor, a painting somewhat theatrical, perhaps, insofar as the figure of Jesus is concerned, but nonetheless striking and full of mystery.

∞

Turning our gaze with Jesus toward the Mount of Olives we must concentrate upon three points: at its foot, Gethsemane; on its slopes, not far from the summit and facing Jerusalem, a place where Jesus used to halt on His way to Bethany with His disciples, a place that still echoes with sublime discourses; and at the top, the place of the Ascension.

Gethsemane means, almost certainly, "oil-press." It was an enclosed part of the great olive plantation which covered the whole of the mountain; and as in the vineyards of Judea for the grapes, so here a press has been installed to deal with the olives that have been gathered. Here was abundant shade. Here under the trees with their silver foliage one might find solitude or repose, and during the fine weather one might even pass the night in the open air.

It was a somewhat gloomy spot. Situated "at the roots of the mountain," as St. Jerome writes, it was only a little raised above the level of the Kedron valley. It was dominated by the lofty walls of Moriah and the pinnacle of the Temple. The tower of Antonia looked on menacingly from a distance, and to the left was the valley of Jehoshaphat with its tombs.

Jesus was accustomed to withdraw to Gethsemane when He needed a secure retreat; the gloomy surroundings soothed Him. He would pray there, far removed from all disturbance, and surrounded only by a few intimate friends whom He could keep at a distance if He willed. Thus it was in nature, in solitude, in the shady gloom, as well as in His Father, that His human infirmity took refuge.

Sometimes He would decide to spend the night there, when He had left the city at a late hour or when He had been long at prayer. Then Gethsemane became a sacred dormitory, and the disciples were privileged to assist at the mystery of Jesus falling into the gentle unconsciousness of sleep while He still kept infinity in His heart. God condescended to lie there resting by the trunk of a tree, His head upon His arms, with His disciples stretched here and there about Him — they, poor mortals, sunk deep in nothingness while He kept heavenly vigil — and John, no doubt, huddled close against his Master, his cheek resting upon His cloak.

But the day was to come when Jesus would be there alone, unable to rest His wearied heart upon the soul of the Twelve.

⚬∞⚬

Higher, and not far from the summit, was another familiar spot. It was a mere halting place, but it was possible to linger there in shelter, for there was a cave near by. Tradition has given to this cave the name of the "Cave of the Teaching." It was known that Jesus stopped there one evening on His way up to Bethany, and, turning toward the Temple, foretold its ruin. On that same occasion He described the end of the world, concluding with long moral exhortations.[163]

As for the place of the Ascension, this is not exactly determined in Scripture. St. Luke places it in the neighborhood of Bethany;[164] the Acts on "the mount that is called Olivet, which is nigh Jerusalem, within a Sabbath day's journey."[165] The crest of the mountain, some distance back, corresponds roughly to these indications, and it is here that we shall seek the divine traces.

⚬∞⚬

As we have said, Jesus contemplates all things in a twofold spirit of prophecy and remembrance because He sees from the

[163] Mark 13:3-27.

[164] Luke 24:50-53.

[165] Acts 1:12. "A Sabbath day's journey" was the distance which one might travel outside the town without breaking the Sabbath. This distance was two thousand cubits, about eleven hundred yards.

viewpoint of eternity. What is, what was, and what will be are equally present to Him. Thus just as upon the Cenacle He projects the vision of the Supper which is past and that of Pentecost which is to come, so on the Mount of Olives He has power to gaze into a double abyss, an abyss of sorrow and an abyss of Heaven.

∞

When Jesus had finished on Mount Zion the Supper which was the memorial of His passing, and when He had explained to His disciples at length the meaning of what He had done, desiring to pursue the matter as they walked, He said, "Arise, let us go hence."[166] The little group set out in the direction of Ophel, crossing the city, at that hour completely deserted. They went down the steep descent toward the ramparts, which they crossed by the Gate of Waters. It is possible, but much less probable that they went by Siloam, passing through the Gate of the Fountain. In any case, either way led to Kedron, to the valley of Jehoshaphat, to the tombs, and to that tomb which is the most terrible of all, the heart's agony.

It was about ten o'clock in the evening. The bright moon of the East, now at its full, bathed the earth with abundant light; the rocks reflected it; the stones of the sepulchers were glistening. The torches of the assassins would be unnecessary, and their swords and staves would be heard plainly in the silence of this night.

Following this same route on the evening of Holy Thursday, in union with Jesus, mingled in spirit with the Twelve, at this same hour, under this same moon of Nisan, certain that he is treading in the very footsteps of the Master — for does he not touch the

[166]John 14:31.

rocks of the narrow path? — the pilgrim can hardly refrain from stooping to kiss the stones of this rocky way. The treason of Absalom had caused this place once to be accursed, and to this very day the Jew or the Moslem casts stones at the traitor as He passes by. But Jesus also has passed by this way, and no curse can survive His footsteps. Absalom was a figure of us. Jesus has wiped away our crimes, and the tears that are shed there, whether they are the tears of Jesus or those of the penitent, have no more bitterness in them.

A few paces up the valley brought them under the great shadow of the pinnacle of the Temple. But the road was brightly lighted, for the moon was high. To their right was the road which led to Moab, the Jordan, and the Dead Sea. The whole of this slope was covered with vines well exposed and in good condition. Jesus takes occasion from these to develop one of His most striking metaphors: "I am the vine; you the branches."[167]

Their progress was slow. They had not far to go and Jesus had much to say, and it is probable that they sat by the way for some time, on some rock or some tomb. There are many natural seats on this path.

After the "tomb of Absalom" and other tombs, like gigantic onlookers that watch the passerby with yawning jaws of night, the path leaves the valley of tombs and leads to the "roots of the mountain." Here is Gethsemane.

It is clear that Jesus has no intention tonight of seeking His usual lodging at Bethany; threatened as He is by His enemies, He will go there no more. His last vigil will not be spent with those dear friends. The Passion has begun, and their next meeting will be at the Cross.

[167]John 15:5.

As is His custom, Jesus enters the garden with the Twelve. At first everything seems to happen as usual, except that Jesus, who normally loves to pray alone, now takes with Him Peter, James, and John, His favorites. He bids the others sit on the grass and wait, as if He intended to return to them soon and continue His discourse, or else to pursue His way up the mountain with them.

And now the great soul which hitherto has shown perfect fortitude begins at last to give signs of disquiet. Jesus is confronted by a horrible vision. So awesome is the sight that He seems to be dumbfounded before horror and fear overcome Him.[168] He reels, and as though unable to remain alone with this nightmare, He communicates it to His disciples, being anxious, perhaps, to explain to them His sudden change of demeanor. "My soul," He says, "is sorrowful even unto death."[169] The "Mighty" of whom the prophet had spoken, the "admirable Counselor,"[170] He who is soon to conquer suffering and death, seems now to succumb; He asks for assistance.

"Stay you here," He begs of them, "and watch with me."[171] He has often spoken of "watching" before, but He did not say "with me." Here is not merely a matter of vigilance; it is pity that the Savior implores.

Then begins that superhuman agony the mystery of which is not revealed to us. At the beginning of His Passion, as at the beginning of His public life, Jesus enters into the wilderness. But the wilderness of His soul, from which He allows all consolation to be shut out, is a bleaker and more fearsome desert than that of John the Baptist.

[168] Mark 14:33.
[169] Mark 14:34.
[170] Isa. 9:6.
[171] Mark 14:34.

He does not merely kneel; He "falls" upon His knees, and lies prostrate with His face to the ground.[172] A chalice is offered Him which He cannot drink. He shudders so violently that the tears pour not only from His eyes but from the whole of His body, bringing with them drops of blood. He weeps with His whole being. He weeps as a man might bleed, and that blood and those tears are for Him the dew of His last night on earth.

Jesus had said, "My soul is sorrowful even unto death." But the words are inadequate; the sorrow of Jesus goes far beyond the bounds of death. Death reaches only the body, and there are limits to what the body can endure. There are sufferings which normally would break the human heart; but God can, if He wills, sustain the soul's frail consort so that the spirit may suffer the more. Death will now stay its hand at the threshold of agony, but for the soul there will be no limit. Chalice upon chalice will be offered Him, until the very Cross will come as a welcome relief. Who shall enter into these depths, and who shall describe how, after those tears of blood that redden the ground, a still more copious flood of tears bathes that soul divine, like a current that flows in the depths of the sea?

We can never comprehend this vision of Jesus, but we may infer it. In the foreground appears death with its retinue of pain and suffering. The Cross has suddenly reared itself before Him. Admittedly the Cross is familiar to His thought, and He has accepted it from the beginning. He speaks of the morrow as "His hour," saying, "For this cause came I unto this hour."[173] But do we not all know the suddenly vivid horror that a prospect may assume after long habit has dulled its outlines? When pain is all-absorbing and the whole mind is concentrated upon its image, then the torture exceeds all bounds. So it is with the Son of Man.

[172] Mark 14:35.
[173] John 12:27.

"My heart is troubled within me: and the fear of death is fallen upon me. Fear and trembling are come upon me: and darkness hath covered me."[174] So far as words can convey, these expressions of the Psalmist give a faithful picture of the agony of Jesus. He is scourged by His thoughts and crucified by His knowledge of what is to come. His visions drag Him across the garden, up the slope to the house of Annas, to the lodge of Caiaphas, to the tower of Antonia, along the streets to death and to the tomb. He sees it all; and for a moment He is seized with an obsession that He cannot shake off. Flat on His face, arms extended, He tastes the extreme bitterness of desolation.

Widen the horizon a little, and still without allowing any consoling reflection to enter in, what do you see? No longer merely the Cross of Jesus, but a multitude of others. Just as in the valley of Jehoshaphat tombs are added upon tombs in endless tiers on the surrounding slopes, so upon this inner Calvary of Jesus and in the landscape around Him, cross is piled upon cross. They press upon and jostle one another: crosses of every size, of every kind of wood. Some are straight, some are bent, others are lying on the ground, rotting like dead trees. The dreadful forest covers mountains, fills the valleys. The very ocean is filled with them, an immense fleet borne upon sobs and sighs.

The Son of Man is come to adopt man, and He takes as His own all the burdens of His sons. His pain is not His own; it is the pain of the whole world. He will overcome our pain by suffering it as by dying He will conquer death. He clings to our sorrow more

[174]Ps. 54:5-6 (RSV = Ps. 55:4-5).

closely than it embraces us, and by His compassion extracts from it all its bitterness.

But if this compassion is to profit us, Jesus must win another victory by His suffering. There is something more terrible than the Cross; it is that which has reared the Cross. Punishment is an effect, of which sin is the cause, and — none can deny it — man is a sinner.

Let us not shrink from words, let us not allow an easy complacency to hide from us the verdict of eternity. Eternity is the true judge; eternity knows what time is worth, and condemns it. Mankind is gone astray; "the whole world is seated in wickedness," says the Apostle.[175] So it is no wonder that our Brother, who has taken our debt upon Himself, feels as He makes spiritual payment the horror which the Psalm expressed in His name: "The sorrows of Hell encompassed me."[176]

He has taken all iniquity upon Himself alone. "He became sin for us,"[177] and now it is no longer Adam that stands before the tribunal, it is the new Man.

Jesus is He who "beholdest the depths";[178] and the greatest depth of all is the depth of moral evil. He feels Himself weighed down beneath the sin of all the ages, like the giants of the fable beneath their mountain. The load saps His strength, and the joint effort of all faithful souls will be needed in order to lighten this hideous burden.

Jesus is the physician who heals our ills with His own pain; but the greatest pain of all is His diagnosis of man's sin. He has a power of vision denied to us; our infirmity closes our eyes to the spectacle

[175] 1 John 5:19.
[176] Ps. 17:6 (RSV = Ps. 18:5).
[177] 2 Cor. 5:21.
[178] Dan. 3:55.

that meets His gaze. Jesus sees wickedness and misery in this world which is hidden from our sight. If each one of us could see all the agonies and all the atrocities that fill the earth, who could live? If we could each see our own self face-to-face, who would dare to show himself?

Our power of self-deception is our protection; but the Seer has no protection, so long as He has no recourse to the one Power that can conquer evil.

∞

And now Jesus turns His eyes to this Power, striving to take comfort in the consideration of its effects.

Jesus came from Heaven to make this world a paradise. But is He not tempted to feel that He has cast Paradise into the mud of the human race? His consolation would consist in balancing the Cross against all this pain and sin, and in seeing that the Cross is heavy enough to countervail it all. But suppose that the Cross itself were a failure? . . .

Of course, it will be nothing of the kind; the Cross is the most powerful weapon for victory. But we have said that the vision of Jesus at the moment contains nothing but pain. In these conditions, will not even victory itself, because of its relative character, appear to be a disaster?

The general who counts only his casualties, the prisoners and the material that he has lost, the positions that he has not taken, the chances that remain to his enemy, and compares his small achievement with his vaster plan, has no sense of triumph. If he confines himself to such calculations he loses the fruit of his victory; in fact, if he is very ambitious, he will regard his victory as a reverse. For is it not a reverse to have done something which is not enough?

The Savior's ambition is insatiable. For one soul He would give the whole of His blood and the whole of His heart. But precisely for that reason, when a soul is lost, even a single soul, He feels that to save it He would leave and forget all the others. His parable tells us so: "If a man hath a hundred sheep, and one of them should go astray: doth he not leave the ninety-nine in the mountains, and go to seek that which is gone astray?"[179]

And how many sheep are gone astray, for all the blood on the shepherd's crook! The Cross is planted in the earth as a rallying point for the human race. How many gather around it and how many turn aside? No one knows, and a wide margin is left for hope. Those who are not in the visible fold have perhaps found shelter in the invisible; those who are scattered in time may perhaps be assembled in eternity. The end of ends is hidden from all of us, and it is an insoluble problem whether the number of the elect be great or small. What is certain is that there is a Hell and that there are people in it — while Jesus is the purveyor of Heaven.

Furthermore, Jesus is the organizer of the earth. He has a plan of life for communities, for cities, for civilizations, and for the generations to come. He does not care for external forms; but the essential relations between men depend upon the ethical doctrine which He teaches and upon the end which He assigns to the whole of the human order.

What will become of this plan? What trace will the Cross leave in history? How much better or more numerous than others will Christian peoples be?

All this is a dark mystery. The work is laborious, and the results, even where tangible, are so slow, so intermingled with checks and reverses that one is tempted to wonder what will be the eventual

---

[179]Matt. 18:12.

outcome. What a cruel vision for Him who is come "to cast fire upon the earth"![180]

Finally, multiply these sufferings by one another. Imagine this body in its sweat of blood, His soul a prey to weariness and to the presentiment of horrors to come, a heart stricken by His children's refusal to love Him, His energy exhausted by the apparent futility of effort — and then say how far torment can go.

Jesus plunges His soul with a cruel delight into this bitter sea of sorrow. He has no hope of alleviation, for He is His own tormentor. The Gospel tells us more than once that "He troubled Himself."[181] He is allied with the whole universe in the attack upon Himself and His soul is dark indeed.

There is no question here of any moral frailty. Jesus has the will to suffer, or rather, He humbly accepts His suffering in accordance with the plan of redemption. Jesus will suffer every kind of pain and sorrow; and what His enemies, who can reach only His body, cannot inflict, He inflicts upon Himself.

∞

Where are the Twelve?

The main group has remained near the entrance to the garden, and they will still be there when the band arrives to take its prisoner.

As for the other three Apostles, the chosen ones, those whom Jesus had made confidants of His own frailty, whom He had humbly besought to console Him, they are at "a stone's cast,"[182] a distance of perhaps forty yards, sufficiently close to hear the groans

[180]Luke 12:49.
[181]John 11:33.
[182]Luke 22:41.

and to realize the exhaustion of their suffering Master. And they are asleep.

Only once in His life has Jesus asked for the help of men, and He does not receive it.[183] These three, Peter and the two sons of Zebedee,[184] whom He has associated with every important step in His public life, whom He has made the partners of His secrets, who alone witnessed the raising of the daughter of Jairus and the Transfiguration, to whom He has but now given so touching a proof of His confidence by allowing them to see His human infirmity: these three forsake Him.

Not only do they fail to assuage His grief; they do not even understand it. The whole drama is enacted between Jesus and Heaven; indeed in the early stages, between Jesus and Himself, left by Heaven to bear His own torment. Vainly He falls to the ground, rises again in quest of help, and once more falls prostrate. Nowhere does He find repose, least of all among men.

And this dereliction is also a part of the chalice which He has to drink. Jesus, accursed for our sakes, must bear the curse by Himself, alone; the traitor might watch but His friends are asleep. What remains for Jesus, seeing that His friends are asleep and His enemies on the watch, but to put Himself entirely in the hands of His Father?

This is what He does. Yet He is disturbed at the thought of this guilty sleep, and setting aside all thought of succor for Himself He thinks of His children. He reproaches them tenderly: "Could you not watch one hour with me?"[185] In the Gospel according to St. Mark we hear the reproach addressed directly to Simon Peter:

---

[183]Cf. Pascal, *Le Mystère de Jésus*, in *Pensées*, no. 736 in *Oeuvres complètes*, ed. Jacques Chevalier (Paris: Gallimard, 1954), 1312-1313.

[184]Matt. 26:37.

[185]Matt. 26:40.

"Simon, sleepest thou!"[186] He calls him Simon, as he was called in the days before he was an Apostle, when he was not the "Rock."[187] Poor Rock! Poor Simon, always presumptuous and always weak!

This detail is mentioned only by St. Mark. The others do not name Peter as the special object of reproach; but Peter names himself through his interpreter, and Mark has no mercy on Peter because Peter has no mercy on himself.[188]

Speaking once more in the grave tone of exhortation that was habitual to Him, Jesus urges His disciples to be vigilant. It is now for their sake, not for His own. "Watch ye and pray that ye enter not into temptation."[189] He says "into" temptation, as though temptation were a trap into which they might fall unawares. He reminds them that the spirit is willing but the flesh weak.

Finally, having left them twice, when He comes back to them for the third time He seems to mingle a sad irony with His reproach: "Sleep now and take your rest. It is enough; the hour is come; behold the Son of Man shall be betrayed into the hands of sinners,"[190] as if to say to them, "What a time you choose for sleeping, heartless disciples! You sleep while your Master is in agony! Are you not thus conniving with these sinners who are about to crucify Him?"

It is an eternal reproach, which Christians in every age deserve when they forget the perpetual anguish of Jesus in His work and in His Mystical Body. "Jesus will be in agony until the end of the world, and we must not sleep during that time."

---

[186] Mark 14:37.

[187] Matt. 16:18.

[188] M. J. Lagrange, *L'Evangile selon Saint Marc* (Paris: Librairie Le Coffre, 1966), 389.

[189] Matt. 26:41.

[190] Matt. 26:45.

∞

Now Jesus has found the help that He needs. Three times the Man of Sorrows knocks at the one door which always opens to a confident appeal. He prays. "And being in an agony, Jesus prayed the longer."[191]

Three times, after the manner of the Jews in moments of crisis, He has recourse to prayer. He appeals to the tenderness of a Father: "*Abba, Pater,* Father! Thou who art the Father!" And He adds, "All things are possible to Thee; remove this chalice from me."[192] But this cry of distress is modified by a condition: "If it be possible."[193] If the supposition be false, then His attitude is one of complete submission: "But not what I will, but what Thou wilt."[194]

In a word, Jesus puts the Our Father into practice.

His intention is to teach us that prayer is an effort to adapt our own wills to the will of God, not to bend His will to ours. When He has brought His soul to this state of submission, He finds perfect peace.

"Arise, let us go!"[195] His courage has returned. He is back in His Heaven, and now, setting aside the infirmities of time, He is in harmony with the decrees of eternity.

But in His interior wilderness He has received a visit; an angel has appeared to Him,[196] and this brother, like Moses and Elijah on Tabor,[197] must have reminded Him of the glories of the Cross.

[191] Luke 22:43.
[192] Mark 14:36.
[193] Mark 14:35.
[194] Mark 14:36.
[195] Mark 14:42.
[196] Luke 22:43.
[197] Matt. 17:1-5; Mark 9:1-6; Luke 9:30.

Henceforth He presents a firm front to all that the future may bring. Let them arrest Him: He offers His hands. Let them buffet Him: He offers His cheeks. Let them condemn and execute Him: silence and patience will be His only reply. After Judas, anyone may torture Him body and soul; He is ready to suffer any injury, having suffered the traitor's kiss.

∞

From His Cross Jesus looks with the eyes of His soul upon Gethsemane and its leafy retreat. That dream of horror has now become a reality which He accepts with courage, and He is at peace. He asks to meet us in Gethsemane when the hour of terror comes for us.

Has He willed to make this meeting place even more tangible for us by allowing some ancient witnesses of His agony, some of those trees, the most venerable in the world after that of the Cross, to survive after so many generations? We may hope that it is so. Then we may say to ourselves, "It was to these trees that Jesus confided His divine anguish; it was perhaps under one of these enormous roots that He lay prostrate in His agony. These petrified trunks were the columns in the temple of His prayer, and these branches were its roof."

But after all, what does it matter? If "the flesh profiteth nothing,"[198] the bark of an olive tree cannot be necessary. The spirit can find what it seeks wherever it may choose to pursue it. Gethsemane is in our hearts, and there we can find traces of His blood, there we can see the outline of His body marked in the warm dust. The essential thing is to weep as Jesus wept.

[198] John 6:64.

∞

When they had left the room in which Jesus had appeared to them, the risen Christ led His disciples "out as far as Bethany: and lifting up His hands, He blessed them. And it came to pass, that while He blessed them, He departed from them, and was carried up to Heaven."[199]

He had said, "I ascend to my Father and to your Father, to my God and to your God."[200] He could not have implied more clearly, as He had indeed expressly told His disciples so many times, that His lot is ours, and that the effect of His sorrows and the effect of ours is the same.

What tenderness is in those words, issuing from such lips in this moment of His solemn departure, as He stands on the brink of the mysteries of Heaven: "My Father and your Father, my God and your God!" It is true, then, that we have only one Father, we and He, that we are members of one divine family, and that He is using no figure of speech when He says that in returning to the bosom of His Father He is going to "prepare a place" for us![201]

There is an ascension for every man; at least there is one prepared for him. At first it will be a spiritual ascension; then at the end of ages it will be like that of Jesus. "The first fruits of them that die"[202] leads His brethren in His train; the "Head" whose body we are,[203] goes up into Heaven, and His members will follow Him.

Let us beware of understanding the words *Heaven, Ascension,* and *departure* in too material a sense. It is vain to dream foolish

[199] Luke 24:50-51.
[200] John 20:17.
[201] John 14:2.
[202] Cf. 1 Cor. 15:20.
[203] Eph. 4:15.

dreams, thus giving occasion to ridicule; our great spiritual realities will gain nothing thereby. The tiny mountain that Jesus now beholds is very little in proportion to the universe. When He leaves it where will He go? And what of the man in the antipodes, what of the astronomer, aghast at the vision of the stars?

No, all this is to a great extent figurative. Jesus goes up in reality before the eyes of His disciples; but the course of His rising is not governed by the plumb line. The clouds do not support Him for long, and even space counts for little in this matter, for Heaven is more especially a state than a place. If we consider only the soul, is Heaven anywhere? And if we consider the body, or the soul in its union with the body, is not Heaven, in which we reign with God, identical with the kingdom of God?

Physically speaking, therefore, Heaven would be the universe, while spiritually Heaven is God Himself and the state of the soul which communicates Him to us. With God, the living Heaven, we are put in accord by thought and love. With the other Heaven, with the whole of creation, we are able to harmonize ourselves by means of the new gifts and the new properties which the risen Jesus has already made manifest. Eternal life makes the body as well as the soul akin to the pure spirit; "the spiritual body"[204] of which St. Paul speaks is the proof of it.

Let us set aside these material dreams, even in that ethereal form in which they may have some incidental interest for us. "The entire beauty of the Lord," says the Liturgy, "is loftier than the stars, and His majesty beyond the clouds of Heaven." Jesus goes up

[204] 1 Cor. 15:44.

6

The Passersby

A landscape does not consist merely of inanimate objects. Places,
dwellings, palaces, and temples have personal occupants; human
life circulates within them. When from the Tree of Redemption
Jesus gazes upon His surroundings and receives the impression of
them upon His mind, the inner picture portrays various persons
who, whether as categories or as individuals, have their importance for us.

Before they nailed Him to the Cross, the Man of Sorrows was
Himself a passerby, one who passed from the praetorium to Golgotha exhibiting His pain, and if we wish to understand His
thoughts we must follow Him along this path.

There are three roads which Jesus may have taken from the
tower of Antonia. From our present point of view it matters little
which of them He took. All three are rough and encumbered; any
of the three might be walked in little more than half an hour at an

ordinary pace, although the obstacles would make the journey much longer.

It must be remembered that we are in an oriental city, on the eve of a festival, with people arriving for the occasion by tens of thousands. The streets are crowded and at certain points and at certain times almost impassable. Then the procession is forced to wait, until the mounted centurion at the head of it has made way with the point of his lance through the beasts and the people that throng the path.

In the East, of course, there is complete fraternity between men, women, children, asses, and camels. Riders jostle pedestrians; people loaded with heavy burdens and ordinary passersby share the narrow space between them as best they can. There are no police in the sense in which we understand the word, and cries, blows, and patience are the sole instruments of order.

This traffic, always a subject of amazement to the modern westerner, is described for us in the letter of Aristeas, an Alexandrian Jew who wrote a few years before Christ. He speaks of the terraced streets which, in Jerusalem as in Jaffa or any other busy town, are like the beds of torrential rivers, surging with crowds, sometimes excited, sometimes indolent. He makes a remark which in view of the Passover is rather significant for us. There are, he says, certain passersby who jostle one another, but there are others who hold themselves aloof to avoid contaminating contact. This preoccupation on their part has the effect of concentrating the rabble, and makes the confusion worse than ever.

Add to this the fact that street hawkers, who ply their trade without restraint, occupy a considerable width of the road. The streets teem with water carriers bearing their goatskin gourds, vendors of curious sweetmeats beloved of villagers who are unaccustomed to such luxuries, men selling fresh or dried fruits and sugared almonds, offering their wares on large plates or on wheeled trucks, purveyors of lemonade balancing their tall tanks crowned with goblets, hucksters of every kind, seeking to exploit the wealth of the visitors, and to assure for themselves months of frugal life at the expense of their momentary greed.

The following day is the great Sabbath, and the festival begins that very evening at sunset. Those who have goods to deliver are in a hurry. The organizers of the festival, the officials of the Temple, foreseeing a great multitude, are making their plans and taking steps to cope with the crowds. Purveyors of doves, sheep, goats, and cattle for the sacrifices are driving their herds toward the enclosure.

Visitors are arriving all the time, laden with all the necessities for camping, and they also have beasts with them. The pedestrian finds his legs entangled with whole herds of cattle and the herds are no less confused than he. Progress is not made any easier by the uneven surface of the roads, their sloping steps, with their little sharp and pointed paving stones. Only some parts of the city are paved with those fine red blocks that are found in Roman towns, blocks which were soon to be utilized for altars.

∞

Jesus passes along, and we see Him making His way through these narrow streets, sometimes in the open air, sometimes under arches, advancing with great difficulty, crushed beneath His Cross and His recent sufferings, stumbling every moment over some step that He had not noticed, or against some wall when the procession is pushed aside. The Cross is jolted and the shock sends shudders through His whole body, deepening the gash in His shoulder. Or else it is a runner who collides with Him, a packsaddle or bag that jostles Him, or else one of those enormous swaying loads which the long files of camels balance as they gravely march along.

Jesus is exhausted, but the soldiers do not bother to make a way for Him. They are in a bad temper, these men; they are working overtime, and it is all due to the trouble that these turbulent Jews are always causing. The Romans have no patience with these local quarrels — such it appears to them! — especially when they have to suffer for them; and soldiers always have to suffer for disorders whether it be to prevent them or to suppress them.

It may be that this ill humor had much to do with the brutality of the guards at the Antonia. Their fury continues on the road to Calvary and it persists at the place of execution. O my Jesus, on what little things do Your sufferings depend! Is the impatience of a mercenary to mean an extra torment for You, and must You pay with Your blood because a drink or a game of dice has been delayed?

No, we know that Jesus depends upon nothing, upon no one. All these trivialities are part of a divine plan, and this plan, decreed by God Himself, is carried out with a free and willing obedience, under the sole inspiration of love.

Jesus makes His way through crowds that become more and more dense as He proceeds. It is known that He is to be executed and attractions such as these stimulate base appetites. The multitude that only just now was clamoring for the sentence cannot be indifferent to the spectacle of its execution. The inquisitive, informed of the news, hurry to see the sight. Passersby stop on their way, crowds gather along the walls, and every flight of steps has its group of onlookers.

At the windows of wealthy houses — for only the rich possess them — the blinds are raised and heads appear, or glowing eyes peer unseen through the wooden lattices. At the open doors old women thrust out their noses, even venturing a few paces into the street; old men, squatting at the doorposts with elbows on their knees, rise to their feet to look; urchins wriggle and twist their way through the crowd. And if there comes a turn in the road, what will happen, with all this multitude surging to and fro? And if from a side street a tide of newcomers should press forward as the Master passes, or some herd of cattle or some cavalcade stampede the procession?

Ah! then another shudder will pass through that already shattered frame, destined for more frightful torment still. From His lips will escape a groan, and if the shock is too great, if His foot should chance upon an uneven cobble, it will mean a terrible fall. We know that there were falls. Christian piety has made no mistake, and if it has stopped at three, this has been perhaps more from love of symbolism than from adherence to literal truth.

How often He has to shrink into some doorway or the recess of some arch! He strives to make Himself as small as possible, effacing Himself so far as His cruel load will allow. He avoids what obstacles He can, suffering the rest with ineffable patience. Truly He may say, "I am a worm and no man."[205] Under His Cross He crawls along those narrow, crowded alleys, sometimes blinded by the sun, sometimes groping in the dark, like an ant in a ridiculous but merciless anthill.

O my God, how mean, how common, how cruel it all is! Which is the more revolting for a tender heart, the cruelty or the inglorious humiliation of this journey? One begins to wish that our Savior may pass unperceived, so that He may have some repose; or, if He must suffer, that at least He might be the hero of some drama worthy of His dignity. Do you see the King of Sorrows thrust to and fro in the confused tumult of this Jewish feast, in the midst of all this clamor; beasts pushing His Cross and making Him stagger as He pursues His painful way; the stale odors of the bazaars

---

[205] Ps. 21:7 (RSV = Ps. 22:6).

of the East serving as incense for the eternal sacrifice? Do you realize that the scene of this event is a network of tiny narrow streets? Do you see His lurches and His awkward stumblings as He advances to the death whose effects are divine?

But we must set aside these scruples, which savor of the greatness that is vain. The greatness of this painful way is measured by the moral greatness, the heavenly mercy, the generous love which are manifest as He passes along. There is nothing of the magnificence of a royal progress here.

And it is better so. Is there not something striking in the contrast between these alleys of death and the grandeur of a deed whose fruit is the salvation of the world? Who could arrange on earth a setting that befits the act of redemption? Eternity and immensity have nothing that can symbolize them here.

It is better that our imagination should be shocked into the deeper realities of thought. A false glamour might deceive; this crying contrast recalls us to the truth. Because it is so commonplace our faith understands that it is immense; and we praise God for making this useful detour. An event without ostentation, with no crown but a crown of thorns, a petty misdeed which is an eternal crime: such is the Passion.

◌∞◌

It is not out of place to recall Pascal's speculations on the three orders of greatness: the material, or the greatness of the *flesh*; the intellectual, or the greatness of the *spirit*; and the supernatural, or the greatness of *charity*. "It is absurd," he writes, "to be scandalized at the lowliness of Jesus Christ, as though this lowliness were of the same order as the greatness that He had come to destroy. . . . He gave the world no inventions, He did not reign as king; [we might add: He was not theatrical in His sufferings] but He was humble, patient, holy, holy unto God, terrible to the demons, and without sin. Truly, in the eyes of the heart which sees true wisdom, He came with great pomp and majesty."[206]

What Jesus is during the whole of His life He is also in His Passion. The greatness of His sacrifice is not spatial, political, or aesthetic; it is moral. In the moral order His sacrifice is great in every sense, going deep down to the roots of good and evil, rising to the heights of infinite merit, with an all-embracing efficacy which passes all bounds.

The Way of the Cross may be narrow, but Jesus' path is in the realm of the invisible. His Calvary may be small, but its effects reach the universe.

∞

The crowd that surrounds Him must be divided into sections; and we shall find there types of sentiment by which we may estimate our own.

There are friends, secret or avowed; there are sympathizers, perhaps many, but more reserved and silent than the others. In addition, there are the indifferent, the inquisitive, the scoffers. And finally there are enemies, official or otherwise, in the midst of the turbulent mob.

The friends, who are later to meet at the foot of the Cross, are already following Him; they are the first of the faithful to make the Stations of the Cross. The Gospel mentions one group of these friends, not the most touching group (because the primary object of the Gospel is to instruct), but one which offers to Jesus His last occasion for a moral exhortation. We will turn to them later.

[206]Pascal, *Pensées*, no. 829 in *Oeuvres complètes*, 1342.

Sympathizers cannot be lacking, for there are many whom the propaganda of the Pharisees has not affected, or who have perceived the hate that inspired it. Without proceeding further in the examination of His cause they tell themselves that an injustice is being committed, and they pity its victim.

Strangers, seeing suddenly before them a man streaming with blood and ill treated by a crowd of ruffians, and remarking in Him signs of dignity and gentleness, must surely be moved to compassion. Man is cruel, but sentiments of pity are latent in him, and he is never long without feeling them. Whether he resists contrary passions, or does not even experience them, he is moved — he is a chance friend.

As for the "indifferent," it is another matter. Most of those who can remain indifferent to so poignant a drama wear their indifference only as a mask. They are potential enemies, or even already enemies in part, unless their selfishness is so great as to absorb the whole of their thoughts. The merchant whose ambition is entirely directed to glittering gain or profitable investments, the coquette described by a Psalm as "adorned all around after the similitude of a temple"[207] — these for the moment may be neither cordial nor hostile. They pass, and they continue to play even in the presence of death.

Yes, Jesus brushed shoulders with luxury, with the life of passion, on His way to death. There was no hatred there, nor even, to all appearances, any complicity in His death. Yet we know that those who continue to dream of trifles when Jesus is passing are His murderers at heart.

The scoffings and the insults related in the Gospel are only examples. The popular imagination is fertile; buffooneries pass

[207] Ps. 143:12 (RSV = Ps. 144:12).

quickly from one to another with commentaries added on the way. Mockery and defiance are hurled without ceasing at one who appears to be utterly powerless and therefore an easy prey for the instinctive cowardice of the mob: "The wonder-worker is meeting a sorry end. . . . A nice sort of healer! . . . Why could he not save himself, since he saved others! . . . If God were with him would He leave him in this plight? . . . Let God deliver him since He is his father! . . . Isn't this the man who was going to destroy the Temple and rebuild it in three days?"

Others are less subtle and do not even trouble to borrow the popular arguments of the doctors of the law. They simply shrug their shoulders: "What is it?" "Oh, nothing: just a slave they are punishing for some crime or other; they are hastening the execution because of the Sabbath; some imaginary king — you can read his titles on the board he is carrying; a quack doctor, a self-styled benefactor, an unbalanced reformer, a redresser of wrongs, an agitator, a dangerous man. It is nothing, nothing. . . ."

Nothing, indeed. It is the Nazarene and the Messiah, who was foretold by the prophets, whom Moses foreshadowed, whom the Psalmist sang of, and whom John the Baptist welcomed at the gates. It is the mysterious man before whom all things trembled before they revolted, and who one day will cause all things to tremble again: revolt, indifference, and hatred — keeping only love. It is nothing, only the Savior of mankind. It is nothing, only the Son of God!

The disciples said on one occasion, "Master, the multitude throngeth Thee!"[208] meaning that they crowded around Him to profit by His goodness. Now the multitude throngs Jesus, but with brutal indifference for a man who suffers, or with cruelty for a man

---

[208] Mark 5:31.

whom they hate. If the first of these two sentiments revolts us, what must we think of the second?

It is probable that many dignitaries demeaned themselves by mingling with the escort, and even encouraging the hostility of the crowd. We find them at Calvary; they had doubtless accompanied their victim. It is a double opportunity for them: to receive salutations, such as Jesus had reproached them with courting, and by contrast to humiliate their conquered foe. Avid of honor they are prodigal of insults; they call for homage and pour out disdain.

At their instigation outrages are committed without restraint. Doubtless they cast stones and dust at Him, as once they were cast at David: this is the oriental way of showing scorn. The writing on the board arouses interest, and the King of the Jews is taunted with not having seen to His own defense. Woe to the man of ambition who cannot gain the upper hand! The caged bird, as soon as it falls ill, is attacked by the beaks of its healthy comrades; even from a tiny bird, cruel man learns a lesson.

Meanwhile the procession has reached the bottom of the hill and now begins the ascent. Jesus is so overcome with fatigue that His progress has now become a piteous stumble. He totters so feebly after His frequent falls that it becomes clear that He cannot go much further. Seeing Him thus, so weak and yet so patient, silent as the flocks of pallid sheep that brush past Him at every moment, one cannot help recalling the words of the prophet: "He shall be led as a sheep to the slaughter, and shall be dumb as a lamb before his shearer."[209]

[209] Isa. 53:7.

It is at this moment that guards find help in an unexpected passerby. They are becoming anxious; the Cross is obviously too heavy and the victim is on the point of collapse. If the sentence is to be carried out the man must be helped in some way, and on the other hand none of them would himself undertake to carry the gibbet of a slave. Never mind! They have the right to requisition help, and they exercise it. So much the worse for Simon of Cyrene, for having chanced this way as he returns from the fields.[210]

A happy chance, indeed, which made Simon and his sons everlasting symbols! Simon, Alexander, and Rufus[211] are honored as saints because the first of them took upon his shoulder the Tree of Salvation and absorbed its life-giving sap. When the soldiers constrain him to carry the Cross behind our Lord they know not the honor they confer upon him. The Romans see in it a minor public service. The Jews find in it a means to husband the strength of their victim. But posterity will find here a subject of praise and meditation to occupy men for all ages.

An ancient painter has depicted the carrying of the Cross as a procession composed of the whole of religious humanity; the leaders of this universal group — the Pope, bishops, and abbots, all wearing their garb of office — are helping the Savior to carry His Cross. They are representatives; in their person we are all collectively Cyreneans, and every individual must be a Cyrenean in his own life. Must we not "fill up what is wanting to the Passion of Christ"?[212] If the Master totters beneath His load, the strength which we have received from Him cannot be better employed than in His service. And in the case of each of us, as in the case of Simon, the help that we give is rewarded a thousandfold.

[210] Matt. 27:32; Mark 15:21; Luke 23:26.
[211] Mark 15:21.
[212] Col. 1:24.

∞

The Gospel mentions a group which was not, like Simon, passing by chance, a group which was following the procession, or at any rate had joined it by one of the roads that crossed the route. It was a group of women. These were not the women mentioned after the crucifixion, those who came from Galilee with Jesus in company with His disciples, but others, who had been attracted by His person or by His doctrine, or else perhaps some of those charitable women who assumed the task of succoring condemned criminals by preparing the narcotic potion for them or performing other services. The Talmud assigns this role to the distinguished women of Jerusalem, and it is certain that it was performed in the case of Jesus, although He did not accept their ministrations.

These Jewish women, as they hail the passing of the pitiful King of the Jews, give a poignant meaning to the words of the Canticle: "Go forth, ye daughters of Zion, and see King Solomon in the diadem wherewith his mother crowned him in the day of his espousals."[213] It is indeed a strange crown that Jerusalem sets upon the head of her king! He should rightly be greeted with lamentations, as the sovereign of old was welcomed in triumph. The inscription, too, which Pilate had invented probably in ironical contempt for the Jews, is appropriate.

The women beat their breasts as a sign of mourning and lamentation over Jesus as He passed along. Their sentiments were good; in their person charity made its appearance upon this scene of bloodshed. But the Teacher of the world will not allow this last opportunity to pass without giving an austere lesson. He had kept silence before His insulters, the indifferent, and the inquisitive;

[213] Song of Sol. 3:11.

His enemies He had met with a calm dignity which disconcerted them. "To pigs and dogs," says an ancient commentator, "you give no answer." And yet to those whose dispositions make them His friends, Jesus speaks.

He is no longer weighed down by His Cross; He can turn to the group and address a few words to them. His executioners seem to raise no objection; in every country it is customary to allow the condemned criminal some little freedom. Nothing but a ferocious hatred can forbid the expression of a final thought, and if hate dominates the Jewish leaders, it has not affected the soldiers.

"Weep not for me," says Jesus.[214] He does not repulse their feelings of compassion, but He deplores a blindness which weeps for effects and overlooks the cause, which pities a noble victim without heed for the much worse fate of His murderers, which forgets that those who strike Him are their kindred — by a mysterious kinship, but a kinship so intimate that it threatens every member of the weeping group. For these murderers are their children.

"Weep not for me, but for yourselves and for your children."[215] Jesus speaks to them of their children, sure that thus He will touch their hearts. He calls their attention to the collective crime which is being committed in Jerusalem, a crime for which Jerusalem will atone with terrible punishment in the future. "Behold, the days shall come, wherein they will say: Blessed are the barren, and the wombs that have not borne, and the paps that have not given suck." So great will be the tribulation that men will curse life itself: "Then shall they begin to say to the mountains: Fall upon us; and to the hills: Cover us."[216]

[214]Luke 23:28.
[215]Ibid.
[216]Luke 23:29-30.

"For," adds the divine Savior, "if in the green wood they do these things, what shall be done in the dry?"[217] If God in His wrath seems to burn and chastise without regard to merit, if He suffers the innocent to be slain, what will He do to the guilty? I die of my own free will in the fulfillment of my task. The end of that task will be a glorious one, and there is no need to weep over a hero who in three days will taste the fruits of His victory. But weep, by all means weep, for yourselves, you who are mothers of deicides; weep for your children who are sneering on the brink of doom.

Let us take a wider view, and let us understand that if Jesus says first, "Weep for yourselves," and only afterwards, "weep for your children," it is because He has in mind an order of events which involves the responsibility of every individual. He speaks expressly of the deicides, but also implicitly of their distant accomplices. And it is these — that is, each one of us — who must take to heart the warnings of His merciful severity.

Tradition introduces at this point two other women, two other passersby: Veronica, with her cloth, and that great passerby whom the Gospel does not yet mention, but whom it would be surprising not to meet until the Cross.

Veronica! the woman with the merciful cloth; the woman who comforts her God; the woman who sets tender and trembling hands to the countenance of Him who said, "He that seeth me seeth my Father also";[218] the woman who wipes away the redeeming blood and draws redemption from its living source; the woman who carries with her the face of Jesus to her home!

[217]Luke 23:31.
[218]John 14:9.

∞

That Mary was present at this point is not a tradition; it is nothing more than a conjecture, a conjecture which rests really upon no positive evidence, any more than does the appearance of the risen Christ to His mother, or her communion in the supper room. But we know that the Gospels are not complete accounts, and every one is at liberty to fill in details suggested by his piety, so long as credence is not demanded for what history does not attest. Still more ought we to respect, and with still greater profit shall we accept, such conjectures as are based upon general sentiment and are adopted by the Church.

It is difficult to imagine that Mary did not watch the cruel procession as it passed, that she was content to await its arrival at the Cross, and that her heart remained unmoved at the thought of her Son's hazardous progress along that piteous way.

Other women are there, and Jesus speaks to them. Can we suppose that Mary is absent? Will she not rather risk all the jostlings and all the insults that may await her? Will she not submit to being tossed to and fro in the crowd like a straw in the wind? If they recognize her, surely they will have compassion! Hers is not the grief that men insult. And if she is able to pass unrecognized, then perhaps they, He and she, may have the cruel comfort of exchanging a glance.

How she envies the Cyrenean! How she, too, would like to carry the Cross! She cannot; but how willingly she would attempt the impossible!

∞

In the Middle Ages one of the churches of Jerusalem was dedicated to this meeting. It was called "Our Lady of the Swoon," or the church of the "Meeting of Jesus with His Holy Mother." Traces were found of a still earlier church, of the fifth or sixth century, among them a fragment of mosaic representing a pair of sandals. It was concluded by some that the feet of our Lady or of her divine Son had left an imprint on this spot.

The conclusion was hasty. It was not uncommon in ancient times to use sandals in this way to symbolize the presence of a person, and often for motives quite unconnected with religion. And even when the symbol was adopted for religious purposes it did not generally indicate a miracle.

Such subtleties apart, however, we may profitably meditate upon the glance which was exchanged between Jesus and His mother. Raphael has given us a moving picture of it in the *Spasimo di Sicilia*. Jesus has fallen beneath His Cross; His executioners are striking Him; He is rising painfully but heroically beneath the blows, and facing Him, also fallen beneath the shock of her emotion and stretching out her arms in distress, is His mother, her whole life striving to express itself in her glowing eyes. The scene has not the majesty of the "Stabat Mater."[219] Here we have only the Mother's tenderness, to which the Savior responds by consenting to her partnership in His suffering. For does not the life which He offers belong in some sort to her who gave it?

It is possible that the meeting of Jesus and Mary took place at one of the crossroads of the Way of the Cross. If not, then it may have occurred at the Gate of Ephraim, where the open space made it possible to stand without fear of opposition from the authorities

[219]Traditional Latin Hymn: "The Sorrowful Mother Standing There."

or of molestation from the crowd. In that case we are nearly back at the Cross once more; and the episode reminds us that we must return to our observation post and continue to contemplate from the Cross the spectacle of our passersby.

∞

City gates in the East are essentially public places where crowds often assemble. In the interior of the city it is rare to find open spaces. Ancient cities carefully avoided them, because the requirements of defense rendered it advisable to reduce the area of the city as much as possible, in order to save the expense of long walls and of numerous troops to man them.

The gates, then, are the ordinary meeting places of the city. Loungers and newsmongers come here in quest of the latest rumors. People requiring information or wanting to do business (such as buying or selling, hiring labor, negotiating marriages) come to the city gates and remain there for a long time. Markets are held here on fixed dates, but every day the gates are the scene of private business deals, accompanied by interminable haggling. It is here at the gates that contracts are signed in the presence of the elders, legal disputes settled, and justice administered — or at least demanded.

The gate is the sign of defensive strength against the outsider; it is also the sign of public authority over the citizens themselves. "The Gate of Kings" signifies the power of kings; and we still speak of the *Sublime Porte* ("the Beautiful Gate"). Jesus used the same symbol when He said of His Church, "The gates of Hell [that is, the powers of Hell] shall not prevail against it."[220]

---

[220]Matt. 16:18.

Politics are discussed for the most part under the arch and in its neighborhood. The opposition has its place here, too; here plots are hatched; rumors are circulated. It is here that Absalom sets his trap to overthrow his father David;[221] it is here that Athalia is slain.[222] The gate is the market and the forum of the cities of the East.

Consequently religion, by reason of its close union with the life of the people, is also associated with the gates of the city. Religion must take its adherents where it finds them. When Israel is unfaithful to Yahweh she sets up on her gates little sanctuaries, "high places,"[223] which are seen perched above the arch, like our statues of the Blessed Virgin. When Israel returns to her God, or to help her to return to Him, the prophets appear at the threshold of the gates, fulminating their prophecies where they will be heard by all the people.

In the book of Proverbs, Wisdom is represented as clamoring at the gates, as well as at the crossroads.[224] It is at the gate that the angel meets Lot when he comes to announce the destruction of Sodom.[225] How often has Jesus healed the sick there, and preached the words of God! And now He is brought here to die, because the place which is in theory — if not in practice — the place of justice is also the place of execution. If justice itself, out of regard for its ministers' comfort, soon took to the shelter of a palace, the sanctions of justice remained faithful to the open air, since the great are not concerned in carrying them out. Moreover, it is important to make an example of the criminal.

[221] 2 Kings 13-20 (RSV = 2 Sam. 13-20).
[222] 4 Kings 11 (RSV = 2 Kings 11).
[223] Lev. 26:30; Num. 21:28; 3 Kings 14:23 (RSV = 1 Kings 14:23).
[224] Prov. 1:21.
[225] Gen. 19:1.

Moreover, the gates are the point of contact between the people of the city and the surrounding country, between one city and another; and the Gate of Ephraim is especially advantageous from the point of view of communication with the outside world. Hence the reason for erecting gibbets here. It is the junction of four of the most frequented highways, and its importance will be shown a few years later when it becomes the forum of Aelia Capitolina, the Jerusalem of the empire.[226] Through here passes a continuous stream of pilgrims, merchants, business people, soldiers, and couriers. The Savior's observation post does not look out upon a desert.

∞

And now look further afield, at Gareb, Bezetha, and still further at the Mount of Olives and Mount Scopus. They are covered with tents and temporary encampments for the use of those who have come up for the festival day. Pilgrims are here from all the lands in which Israelites swarm; for among the Jews the Passover is a universal devotion. They are grouped according to tribes or families — Galileans with Galileans just as we now see Greeks with Greeks on August 15 at our Lady's tomb — all packed closely together. These temporary towns add a formidable contingent to the multitudes that throng the Holy City.

Imagine the spectacle. At the gate itself is a continuous stream of people, flowing between two animated banks of itinerant merchants, with wheeled stalls and permanent booths all along the street offering drinks and sweetmeats for sale, while beggars — especially the blind (numerous in this land of dazzling sunshine),

---

[226]The city was built c. 130 on the site of Jerusalem by the Roman emperor Hadrian (A.D. 117-138).

cripples, paralytics, and lepers more or less healed — raise their monotonous plaint and shake their little wooden bowls.

In the gardens idlers sit squatted on the ground or else astride the walls. On the roads are people, donkeys, herds of cattle, vehicles, and slow-moving camels with their swaying burdens. On the hills are dense masses of pilgrims, animated groups sitting around their fires.

Visualize this scene and listen as Jesus appears and the Cross is raised. There is first a great hum of excitement, then sounds of hostility and shouts of laughter, which for the moment stifle the more timid stirrings of reflection and pity.

"All they that saw me have laughed me to scorn: they have spoken with the lips, and wagged the head. He hoped in the Lord, let Him deliver him: let Him save him, seeing He delighteth in him."[227] Always that cruel blasphemy! Christ is ever "the reproach of men and the outcast of the people."[228]

And yet in that crowd are many indebted to Him, many who previously were His admirers. These crippled beggars and these unhappy wretches had cast themselves at His feet, full of trusting prayers; they acclaimed Him the Son of David. They came to kiss His cloak, to touch its white fringe with the hyacinth border, and prostrate before Him, they had awaited a miracle or a word that would give them hope.

Now they turn from Him, they mock Him and, fulfilling the words of a Psalm which gives the whole story of the Passion, they sing after Him as He passes the gate, drinking as they sing: "I became a byword to them. They that sat in the gate spoke against me: and they that drank wine made me their song."[229]

[227] Ps. 21:8-9 (RSV = Ps. 22:7-8).
[228] Ps. 21:7 (RSV = Ps. 22:6).
[229] Ps. 68:12-13 (RSV = Ps. 69:11-12).

"O all ye that pass by the way, attend, and see if there be any sorrow like to my sorrow!"[230]

∞

Truly, my Master, never has there been sorrow so forsaken, as there has never been sorrow so bitter and so complete. Not only in Jerusalem but in the whole universe, not only on this Sabbath eve when a hated criminal is being hurried off to execution, but throughout the whole course of ages, how many passersby will there be whose hearts are truly moved — and moved to repentance — by this spectacle?

Jesus is not mocked today; but is He not generally forgotten? Compassion is rare, still rarer is active devotion. And when we say that Jesus is no longer mocked we are thinking only of His person, to which Jesus Himself attaches far less importance than to His work and to our salvation.

How many insults are hurled at the doctrines, the practices, the ministers, the precepts, the promises, the words, the deeds, the institutions, and the persons connected with the name and work of Jesus crucified! Here, too, there are those who mock and wag their heads; here, too, are drinkers of wine — the wine of sophistry and licentiousness — who sing after Jesus as He passes.

The Passover of mankind still continues. Men pitch their tents and move on; men drink and dance; men worry and become absorbed in business; men form attachments and break them; men love and hate — and Christ hangs on the Cross. His sorrow meets only with contempt, and His appeal, His offer of salvation, arouses nothing but a vague and distracted smile.

[230]Lam. 1:12.

"All ye that pass by the way," you men who find Christ at some Gate of Ephraim in the course of your life, be it busy or impassioned, unhappy or dissipated, "attend and see if there be any sorrow like to this sorrow," any sorrow so full of significance for yourselves, so worthy of your compassion, so apt to win your love and to guide your lives.

If there be no sorrow like to this, if the chance passerby is forced to acknowledge and to confess despite himself that there is something superhuman here, that this event has a significance surpassing all life on earth, then let him stop and join the band of those "by the Cross,"[231] whom we are now about to study — those who offer themselves to be cleansed by the saving dew that falls from the sacred wounds.

[231] John 19:25.

7

His Loved Ones

"There stood by the Cross of Jesus, His mother and His mother's sister, Mary of Clopas, and Mary Magdalene."[232] At some little distance was another group of friends who looked on, and there were other women, "who had followed Jesus from Galilee, ministering unto Him."[233]

John, too, the first of these two historians, was there. He does not give his own name, but the happy privilege reserved for him will reveal it. It is to him that Jesus will bequeath His mother.

∽

But where are the Twelve?

When Jesus brings His gaze down from the horizon to bear upon the people around Him, when He seeks with His eyes those

[232] John 19:25.
[233] Matt. 27:55.

who "had continued with Him in His temptations,"[234] what does He see? Some women, and that Apostle whose temperament makes him akin to them. The others are far away. One tradition says that they have hidden in the valley of Kedron among the great tombs. More probably they have made their way to the upper part of the city. They are huddled away in some corner, full of terror and distress, awaiting events.

For them the Master is already dead; the "kingdom" is without a king; the school is without a teacher, the family is without a father. They themselves will quote the prophecy in their writings: "I will strike the shepherd and the sheep of the flock shall be dispersed."[235]

In the garden they were asleep. When the iniquitous band arrives and lays hands upon Jesus, one of them makes a bold gesture. He draws his sword and cuts off the ear of one of the enemy, but the resistance goes no further. Jesus makes things so easy for them! He forbids violence; He wants only loyalty. He says to the guards, "I am He; if therefore you seek me, let these go their way."[236] He wants the words of the prophet to be fulfilled even in the temporal sense: "Of them whom Thou hast given me, I have not lost any one."[237]

Thus the disciples may do as they will. The way is open in every direction, and only one path leads to death. Did they suffer reprisals for their attempted defense of the Master? Were they struck by the guards and put to flight? Or, more simply, do they tell themselves that they can do nothing to help, and that they had better save their skins while they can? We do not know. In any

[234] Cf. Luke 22:28.
[235] Zech. 13:7; Matt. 26:31.
[236] John 18:8.
[237] John 18:9.

case, their hesitation is as brief as their decision is unanimous; they take to flight. The serene and kindly acquiescence of Jesus is passport enough.

Yet how sadly He had said, only the evening before, "Behold the hour cometh, and it is now come, that you shall be scattered every man to his own, and shall leave me alone." As if to give them an excuse, He had added, "And yet I am not alone, because the Father is with me."[238] Then, in an excess of kindly compassion, He concludes, "These things I have spoken to you that in me you may have peace."[239] The soul of Jesus is in these words. But should not love have seen in them the final link to bind them to their duty?

Oh, Peter (the "Rock"), Simon (the "Zealot"), Andrew (the "Courageous"), Jude or Thaddaeus (the "Energetic"), James (the "Brother" of Jesus), and you, Matthew, who received the "gift of God," where are you? How will you bear witness to this death, ye witnesses? Can you, without shame, say that you are reserved only for the glories of the tomb? Are you men of the Resurrection, and not men of the sacrifice?

∞

The disciples are not there. Two among them, Peter and probably John also — although his name is not given — took courage again after the general flight. They followed at a distance after the band as it made its way up toward Zion, and entered the house of Caiaphas. In this they were running little risk, for the unnamed disciple was acquainted with the high priest and could therefore make an excuse for his presence.[240] As for Peter, who enters under

[238]John 16:32.
[239]John 16:33.
[240]John 18:15.

cover of his companion, we know what he does. The shadow of danger and the words of maidservants are enough to bring him low. Three times he denies the Master whom he had only just now defended with such rash folly, the Master to whom he had said, "I will lay down my life for Thee."[241]

To all of them Jesus had given increasingly constant and generous motives for loving Him. To what intimacy He had admitted them! Both in their manner of life, and in feeling and thought, their union was as close as it was surprising, given the distance that separated them from Him.

In our western climates the life of a teacher with his disciples is much less intimate than in the family circle. In the East it is more intimate. Teacher and disciples live together as mountain climbers do, like the members of a polar expedition or a caravan in the desert. They eat together in the fields, in a boat, or on the banks of a stream. They sleep in one another's breath, under a rock or in the open air. Grouped around a fire they talk without constraint, and their thoughts are as much in common as the food they eat.

Jesus, a rabbi like the rest of rabbis and humble of heart as none other was in Israel, lent Himself to this life without reserve. He opened His heart to His disciples as much as the capacity of those very human beings would allow. "To you," He said, "it is given to know the mystery of the kingdom of God; but to the rest in parables."[242] "I will not now call you servants: for the servant knoweth not what his lord doth. But I have called you friends: because all things whatsoever I have heard of my Father, I have made known to you."[243]

[241] John 13:37.
[242] Luke 8:10.
[243] John 15:15.

He called them, in fact, His friends, His children, His little children, His little flock. He showed them the indulgence of a mother, the patience and the careful attention of the tender teacher. Having received all, so that He could say to them, "You have not chosen me: but I have chosen you,"[244] they could still quarrel among themselves for the first place beside Him. But He did not scold them. Instead, He took a little child upon His knees, kissed it, and said, "Whosoever shall humble himself as this little child, he is the greater in the kingdom of Heaven."[245]

He anticipated their faults and comforted them in advance, so that they might feel less the gnawings of remorse. And He did this also in regard to their desertion of Him: He raised them up before they fell. But, once again, should not this have been a further motive for their loyalty? Instead, it became their excuse!

∞

But they may rest assured. For all their unworthiness, they need not feel that before the tribunal of the Cross they will be set aside as of no account, or condemned as traitors. Their Master knows them better than they have known Him; He discerns within their hearts that which is hidden from themselves. They are weak, vacillating, selfish, unintelligent — and now they have proven cowards also. But they have believed and have given themselves to Him, and that makes up for everything.

These friends who have tormented Him before His enemies made Him suffer, who have all misunderstood Him more or less, who have fatigued Him with their follies and their demands, who have been a drag upon His footsteps during His apostolic work:

[244] John 15:16.
[245] Matt. 18:4.

these friends — all save one, the traitor — are deep within the Savior's heart.

For Him their goodwill has always been enough. Tomorrow His Spirit will make use of that goodwill to operate a marvelous transformation. He looks at them with the Cenacle in mind; He looks at them thinking of the time, not long ago, when He had called them to follow Him. They had left all things, these men, at His first call, and later, one after another, they will face death for His sake. He will not remark their absence! He regards them all as present in that one of their number who stands by the Cross. With John and with us He will confide them to the care of His mother, and He Himself, more a mother than all the mothers that ever were — even His own — gathers them all to His loving heart, because they are the nucleus of His Church.

They file before His vision: Andrew, the brother of Simon Peter, the man who at the sight of a gibbet like His Master's will cry out "O good Cross!" and James, the son of Zebedee, who declared that he could drink the chalice, and in fact will drink it;[246] Thomas, the doubter, the man who wants to feel, who believes only in tangible proofs, but was nonetheless the first to exclaim as they went up to the city of blood, "Let us go, that we may die with Him!"[247] There is Bartholomew, or Nathaniel, "in whom there is no guile," who in the great Unknown recognized the "king of Israel";[248] Philip to whom it was said, "Philip, he that seeth me seeth the Father also,"[249] and who gazed full into the divine eyes with eyes of faith; Matthew the tax collector, who, called by a gesture as he sat at the receipt of custom, left all things

[246] Matt. 20:22.
[247] John 11:16.
[248] John 1:47, 49.
[249] John 14:9.

and celebrated his vocation by giving a joyous banquet; Thaddaeus or Judas, "not the Iscariot!" says his fellow disciple John fearfully as he names him,[250] and Simon the Cananaean, called the Zealot. These two men will remain almost entirely unknown to us, to shine only by their martyrdom. Lastly there is the other James, the "brother" of the Lord, who will be the venerable support of the young Church, the custodian of its piety and the example of its zeal, until he is cast down from the pinnacle of the Temple, saying with his divine Brother, "Lord, forgive them, for they know not what they do."[251]

And last of all, Peter. Peter, the poor renegade, whose absence from Calvary is perhaps due to shame and to the desire to make reparation rather than to further cowardice; Peter, who is at this moment receiving his baptism of tears; Peter of the feverish eyes and the cheeks furrowed deeper day by day; Peter, whose name is embodied in the landscape of the Holy Land, for who can hear the cock crow at Jerusalem without thinking of his heartbreak, without seeing the silent glance of Jesus, and the unhappy friend as he flees remorsefully into the night?

In Bach's *Passion according to St. Matthew*, Peter's tears are sublime. But they appear to the pilgrim in a more mysterious way when at three o'clock in the morning the cocks of Siloam and the Mount of Olives give out their summons to the light, symbolizing the divine call to repentance and to the light of life.

If Peter were present at the foot of the Cross he would assuredly find in the first glance of Jesus that sad and sweet expression that roused him from his sin in the house of Caiaphas. But in that same glance he would read His forgiveness. Peter's fall earned for him the virtue of humility, the first power of the soul; his martyr's

[250]John 14:22.
[251]Luke 23:34.

129

death, closing a great life, will give proof of his generosity. Peter, too, will be crucified. But he will shrink from the glory of reproducing against the sky the figure of his Master: he will ask to be crucified head downward, thus showing by the same act his lowliness and the completeness of his sacrifice.

Jesus looks upon him, and although Peter is far away he must feel that look, the look which melts the wickedness of the human heart, sees deep down into its love and strengthens its weakness. The Rock has faltered; but it is upon him that the eternal work is founded. Where flesh has shown itself to be frail, the power of God will give strength. Peter fell; but he was the first to believe in Jesus the Son of God, in Jesus the promised Christ. Indeed it is to him that we owe the conjunction of the two words "Jesus Christ."[252] He was the first to call the Savior by His name.

∞

They are present, then, in spirit. They are present by their faith, by their hearts which are devoted to His service, by their vocation which they have not renounced, and by their souls which are loyal to Him. They are absent only by timidity. Jesus blesses them, and as He bleeds for them He pays out the ransom for each. On the morrow He will call them His "brethren,"[253] putting them upon the same footing as Himself now that their common task is to be visibly committed to them, the nations given them for their spiritual heritage, and all generations assured to their descendants.

They will bear witness to Him. Their hearts will be the tables of His law. It will be their task to organize His work of salvation

[252] Matt. 16:16; Mark 8:29; 1 Pet. 1:1.
[253] Matt. 28:10.

and to plant His Cross in every part of the earth. Jesus will make them the foundation of His social edifice, main branches of the great tree, candlesticks to give light to the world, springs to fertilize it, luminaries in the heaven of Christendom.

For, it cannot be denied, the world has been enlightened and made fruitful by these men, and is guided by them even today. A few boatmen, a tax collector, and a carpenter, slow of under-standing, cowards whom grace has strengthened, absent in the moment of crisis yet to us ever present: such are our ancestors. This is the miracle of the Cross: it saves even those who desert it, provided that the heart is not estranged.

They are present, but not in their full number. One is missing. This morning at dawn, when Jesus had been definitely condemned and was about to be led to Pilate, a man made his way to a desert place. He was haggard; he felt dreadfully alone. He looked about him and it seemed to him that all things cast him off. He did not see the glance that is ever awaiting ours, the unseen arms ever stretched out to save.

It was Good Friday, and he failed to understand the meaning of that day. The blood which his treason had set flowing was not in his eyes the fountain of life that asked nothing better than to cleanse him first of all. He hurled his last insult at the love which had chosen him out. He selected a tree in a field, hung his girdle to a branch and tied it fast. Then, passing his neck through the noose, he cast himself into a double abyss of death.

∝∞

Let us leave this unhappy memory; brighter visions await our gaze. If we do justice to the Twelve even in their absence, shall we refuse to honor those who are valiantly present, those who mourn at the foot of the Cross?

The holy women are there, sometimes near the Cross, sometimes at a distance, depending on whether the crowd allows them
to approach. They have followed Jesus on his journeys, and now
that He needs someone to perform the last services for Him they
are still at hand. Their presence is symbolic; it foreshadows the
future and shows the part that woman plays in the life of Christianity, as in the life of Jesus.

Women have an important place in the constitution of the
infant Church. As early as the Galilean ministry, St. Luke describes the group which accompanies the Master: St. Peter in the
first rank, with eleven other Apostles aiding Jesus in His ministry.
In addition, some women, several of whom had been healed of
various diseases or of evil spirits, assist the apostolic band with
their labors and their goods.[254]

In this there was nothing unusual. The Pharisees with their
reputation for piety attracted the religious souls of women; they
received help from them, and no one was scandalized by this. That
the women should follow Jesus in His journeys was perhaps an
innovation; but they removed all difficulties by attaching themselves to His mother.

These women, devoted to Him from the beginning, will be
devoted until the end. They will embalm the tomb; they will be
witnesses of the Resurrection; they will have their part in the
outpourings of the Spirit at Pentecost; they will consecrate themselves to the work of their divine Friend, after having cherished
and adored His person. On Calvary they receive their investiture;
what their sisters will be in the history of Christianity, they are at
the foot of the Cross. Here on Calvary is the authentic picture of
hallowed womanhood.

[254]Luke 8:1-3.

And as the Twelve have a hierarchy in which Peter, James, and John hold the first rank, with Peter at their head, so the holy women have their protagonists in Mary Magdalene, her sister Martha, Mary of Clopas (the mother of James the younger and Joseph), Salome (the mother of James and John and the wife of Zebedee), Joanna (the wife of Chuza, the steward of King Herod), and Susanna. In the first rank of all these is Mary Magdalene, and above and beyond them all, dominating the group, is Mary the mother of Jesus.

These gentle hearts — we leave aside for the moment the unique heart of the Virgin Mother — have understood better than the men all the sublime sweetness and tender strength of Jesus, prophet, Messiah, and martyr. His greatness has won them; His goodness has attached them to His side. His suffering can only bind them closer; it fascinates them.

Woman is essentially a consoler. Her outlook upon life leads her to be a helper because, since she herself is the giver of life, she is more conscious than man of its frailty and its needs. She protects what she has given.

∞

These compassionate souls, at once daughters, friends, and — to some extent also — mothers, are there and weeping bitterly. They strive with their glance to give courage to the Master, and invite Him to share His human weakness with them. At the same time, by confessing Him to be their God and Redeemer, they call down a grace upon themselves: their reward is the commission to tend His burial. Already this body is theirs. One of their number has embalmed it in advance, and soon all will go hastening before the Sabbath dawns to buy spices, that they may envelop in sweet odors the stony couch of Jesus.

∞

And where is she, she who embalmed her Savior in advance, she who anticipated her sisters and poured the first spikenard, provided the first shroud — her own hair — to wrap around the feet that she had bathed in sweet smelling oil and in her tears?

We cannot conceive her otherwise than as prostrate at the foot of the Cross, embracing it with her arms, making herself one with it, and welcoming the blood that flows from it, bedewing her head. In art she will always be depicted thus, unless it be as supporting the blessed Virgin in her moments of direst agony.

She says nothing; what words could express what she feels? She is not even thinking, not even suffering; it is Jesus who thinks and suffers in her. She dares not speak of the oppression in her heart, for she has no heart of her own. In her breast she feels the great palpitations which fitfully convulse the breast of the Martyr. She has no more blood, for the blood of Jesus is flowing; she has no more will, for she has surrendered it to His. For her also "it is consummated,"[255] and now she can only weep.

Mary stands at the foot of the Cross; but Magdalene has not this obligation. Magdalene is not the Co-Redemptress; she is only a loving and suffering soul, plunged in the sorrow of her Beloved and striving to equal His with her own. The scene which took place in Simon's house is re-enacted, but now its significance is apparent, for there is none of the outward glory that before had veiled it.

What a deed that was, and what amazement it aroused in those who failed to perceive its heart-rending symbolism! The meal is in full progress, the Master is in deep conversation with His host,

[255]John 19:30.

134

when — availing herself, it is true, of a recognized custom, but one surely forbidden for a sinful woman! — she enters the room carrying a precious vessel. She places herself behind Jesus, who is reclining at the table in the oriental fashion, and there, alone with her love, ignoring the crowd that watches her, she begins to bathe the head of the guest with spikenard and to anoint His feet with scents. Then letting down the tresses of her hair, she wipes from the sacred feet her perfume and her tears with them.[256]

Perhaps we can understand her action and what impelled her to so bold a deed. She has been raised up from her unworthy life. Her "seven devils" have fled, leaving her with the soul of a child, save that it is more ardent and filled with a boundless understanding. Through Jesus she has at last come to know true happiness. Through Him she has learned not to desecrate love, and the love in her, now cleansed from defilement, wells up the stronger because it has so many mad follies to redeem.

After her blatant sins, must she not show a blatant sorrow? Having in all else braved the eyes of the world, she will brave them now in humility, in greatness of soul, and in faith. So magnificent will she be in her role that she will become a symbol of spiritual resurrection, a patroness of repentant sinners.

But there is another motive that decides her. Jesus is going to die, and she knows it; the intuition of one who loves has revealed to her what is hidden from nearly all others. At the tomb of Lazarus the attitude of Jesus' enemies did not escape her. She who then said confidently, "If Thou hadst been here, my brother would not have died,"[257] might now have said at the foot of the Cross, "Had it not been for me, had I not forced Your tender love, perhaps You, my adorable Master, perhaps You might not have died!"

[256]John 11:2; Luke 7:36-38.
[257]John 11:21.

Yet she realizes that for this death there are wider reasons. She may have provided the occasion, but what of the cause? Jesus is the victim, not only of the Jewish leaders, not only of the friends by granting whose requests He called down upon Himself the anger of His enemies. Jesus is the victim of all human souls.

Yes, Jesus is the victim of every human soul in the measure of the sins of each. This is a further anguish for Magdalene. What horror overcomes her at the thought of her sins! What a sense of her eternal responsibility! It is for her sins that Jesus is paying the price, and if her love comes to her all bleeding, will she not go out to meet it?

And so she makes her entry into the Passion. She anticipates events; she joins Jesus in His knowledge of what is to come, although His knowledge is eternal; she submits; she humbles herself; she weeps; she gives thanks — and between the two is a sort of secret complicity, of which Jesus gives only a hint for the instruction of His host: "She hath done what she could: she is come beforehand to anoint my body for the burial."[258]

And as a result the perfume poured out there will embalm the world, as the Body risen from the tomb will fill it. As Jesus says, "Amen, I say to you, wheresoever this gospel shall be preached in the whole world, that also which she hath done, shall be told for a memorial of her."[259]

The house of Simon that day was like the anteroom of the new sepulcher which is set apart for funeral anointings, and the heart of Mary Magdalene, after that of the Blessed Virgin, was the first tomb. Magdalene mourns Jesus in advance; she mourns Him as one would a newborn baby. For her He is newly born, having just been born in her.

[258] Mark 14:8.
[259] Mark 14:9.

And her vessel? What of the vessel of fine alabaster with the slender neck? She breaks it, for it must serve no other use. Not even for Him will it serve again, for He will die. If only she might cast it into the sepulcher! In the tombs of Canaan we frequently find vessels and other objects broken in homage to the dead.

But since He is to die, and to die for her, will she remain behind? She cannot imitate the Hindu spouse who mounts the funeral pyre of her lord, to mingle her ashes with his. But she does better: by penance, by a total self-surrender, she buries herself as she has buried her Lord, and she submits to death in Him.

At the foot of the Cross she renews her gift, and it is herself, more than her tears and her heart's blood, that she pours at the feet of her suffering Beloved.

At one time she had sat at His feet to hear His words; this was her "part"[260] which was not taken away from her. She rose from His feet only to anoint them in the house of Simon. Now she embraces those feet on the Cross. Tomorrow she will cast herself at those feet again. She cannot leave them, for there she recognizes her own place; there she can give vent to her passion of humility and love. Magdalene is ever prostrate, ever lowly, because love has taken hold of her, and her own life is no more.

∽

"Stabat Mater Dolorosa"

At the Cross her station keeping,
Stood the mournful mother weeping,
Close to Jesus to the last.

[260]Luke 10:42.

Oh, how sad and sore distress'd
Was that mother highly blest
Of the sole-begotten One!

Christ above in torment hangs;
She beneath beholds the pangs
Of her dying glorious Son.

Is there one who would not weep,
Whelm'd in miseries so deep,
Christ's dear mother to behold?

Can the human heart refrain
From partaking in her pain,
In that mother's pain untold?

Only the Liturgy can worthily introduce a theme offered to the meditations of centuries and to the salutary stirring of hearts. The Church loves this picture. One could say that the "Stabat Mater" is the reflection of Herself, that it is Her hymn of maternal woe and suffering glory. The Church has searched the prophecies; She has exclaimed with Jeremiah to Her great ancestor, "Great as the sea is thy destruction: who shall heal thee?"[261] She applies to Mary the Mother of Sorrows as She applies to Jesus what is said of the desolate daughter of Zion: "All ye that pass by the way, attend, and see if there be any sorrow like to my sorrow."[262]

∞

In all things Mary is unique. After Jesus and in Him, by reason of her relations with His sacred person and with His work, she

[261] Lam. 2:13.
[262] Lam. 1:12.

surpasses every creature associated with the fate of mankind, whether in merit or in grief, as also in glory to come.

She is the Virgin, the Mother, and the Co-Redemptress. She is the flower which has opened its blossom only for Heaven. She is the sun that gives us light, the spring that gives us purity, the furrow in which the bread of mankind took growth. It is from you, Mary, that comes the life of the world, because "He that was born for us has chosen to be yours."[263]

It is natural that one who holds this rank will sever herself in time of sorrow neither from the work nor from Him who accomplishes it. What she had not suffered in giving Him birth, says one of the Fathers, she suffers now as He dies. Once she had felt Him live within her; now it is within her that He dies. The infancy, the hidden life, His life of preaching — all these were hers. How much more does the end call for the presence of His mother!

∞

Her present grief is measured by what this Son was for Mary. He was her God, and He was flesh of her flesh. He was part of her, and He was one of the three divine persons. She has fed Him in the name of earth and Heaven; she has lived for Him, who willed to have life from her, and for whom she herself was born. She has watched His earliest tears, smiled at His first words; she has guided His first steps, faltering like our own. She has lifted in her hands the treasure of this soul which gave radiance to our flesh which once was darkness, and in which God manifested Himself.

Of her He expected all, because she was predestined to give all. For many long years He never left her; later she followed Him. We

[263] From the hymn "Ave Maris Stella."

imagine the relations between them during those three years as a mystery that only intimates can relish, but a mystery the sweeter for being so deep. Now He is leaving her; in one day she is losing her God and her child. Her grief is human only because she is human; its object surpasses the understanding of man.

And so the saints see Mary on Calvary as bleeding. She is covered with the blood of her Son, whose wounds she kisses. This blood and her pallor make her a tragic figure, a Niobe more sorrowful than Niobe, but also more tender and more pure, and by reason of her very greatness, most accessible to the hearts of men.

But it is within her soul especially that we must see the Virgin bleeding. She stands at the foot of the Cross, but her heart is nailed to it with her Son and it shares the infinity of His pain. He is the victim of the five wounds; she is the woman of the seven swords. He is crucified; she is transfixed. He suffers the Passion; she the Compassion.

They are united by a common effort which welds them into one. Jesus looks at Mary with the thought that she sees Him suffer, while Mary finds in Jesus the counterpart of her grief. Mutually they afflict each other, mutually they are consoled. He does not keep for Himself all that His humanity endures. That humanity came from Mary: Mary has her rights in it, and Jesus does not refuse her claim.

He allows her to see all, to feel all, taste all: to lie upon the bed of anguish, to be pierced by the nails and torn by the thorns, to labor for breath with the choking, and to feel the terrible cramp that tortures His poor frame. He keeps nothing to Himself; all is reproduced in her. He wills that it should be so; instinctively He desires it.

Instinctively? Yes, instinctively as the son of Mary; for Jesus, like every man in agony, has become a child again. We need not fear to attribute to Christ those endearing weaknesses which He

Himself did not hide in the Garden. If He implored the help of His disciples, He is not unyielding before His mother. He turns His bleeding face toward that countenance upon which He first saw a human smile; the Head made restless by the crown of thorns seeks a soft shoulder for its repose. How He would love a kiss from that mother's lips!

In the past, was it not His joy from time to time to forget that He was a grown man, so that He might return to His mother's bosom? Did He not find here His rest, His ever present Bethany, where He might forget His hours of sadness and relax after the constant tension of His work? The dignity and the sublime manliness of the Son of Man do not seem incompatible with an endearing childlike quality which persists even in the strongest men, and shows itself in moments of suffering.

How willingly she would have received Him in her arms! And how happily would He have cast Himself into them! Soon, when He expires, He will let His head fall toward her and relax His whole body so as to confide it to her care in death, as she cared for it at His birth. This will be her moment: the icy body will be her portion, and then those two bodies, the one scarce colder than the other, will be warmed by one heart alone.

∞

We may also remind ourselves that, although the sorrows of Jesus are incomparably supreme, those of Mary are of longer duration. Mary will suffer the death of her Son, while the Crucified will suffer only the agonies which are its preliminary. She will receive the thrust of the lance that pierced His side; the wounds which she sponges will seem to be alive, and in truth they will be alive in her. The rigid body upon her knees, the head lolling lifelessly on her breast, will arouse quivers of grief in the bosom of her who gave them life. Then — since the Resurrection was as yet hidden behind a cloud — she will live His death again when they take Him to the tomb.

And later, how often will she recall these memories! She will be seen wandering through the streets of Jerusalem, seeking the traces of His sorrowful Way; lingering in the places where He fell; meeting His glance once more at the crossroads or at the Gate of Ephraim; joining the band of women whom He favored with His final discourse; slowly ascending the slope of Golgotha, closing her eyes the better to see, walking in silence the better to hear, and coming finally to the place of the Cross, there to meditate long and deeply.

Then, she will live only in order to love at the price of suffering; now, her whole life is devoted to suffering so that she may love the more. Then, her grief will be prolonged for the sake of the work; now, it is immeasurably intense for the sake of the person, by reason of the bond which unites her with Him.

∞

But surely the work also has its part in the present grief. Mary would not be united with Jesus if she did not consecrate herself, and with herself her grief, to the cause for which He is dying. The Cross is an altar, and the Victim must also find an altar in Mary, the altar of her heart.

For what was she made, if not for that consent which was the proximate cause of the Incarnation, if not for that cooperation which she was subsequently to give? If Jesus is the second Adam, is Mary not the second Eve? She knows her vocation. The sword of Simeon did not await the moment of Calvary. And even before Simeon, was there not the sweet grief of the manger, the exquisite and tragic Annunciation?

It was a crucified Infant that she bore in her womb. Some painters have represented Jesus as descending to the womb of His mother in a ray of light, a child bearing the Cross upon His shoulder. They are right. Mary begets death in order to beget life. The infant's milk is the portent of the gall and vinegar; the poor manger is the first "wood." Jesus Himself will not think it amiss to foretell to Mary these cruel events, which His silent eyes have already betrayed.

Was the intimacy between mother and Son ever peaceful and free from restraint? Happy it was, indeed, but with that austere happiness of heroes who know the weight of their destiny and the formidable price of their glory. Jesus was ever dying, and Mary ever consenting to His sacrifice. She accepted her part, which was to contribute to everything. She had erected the Cross in her will before she saw it on Calvary. In spirit she had buried her Son.

And today she retracts nothing; on the contrary, she intensifies her acceptance. The sorrow of Jesus is voluntary in her as well as in Him. Mary, as well as her Son, might say, "No man taketh my life from me, but I lay it down of myself, . . . and I have power to take it up again."[264] The soul of Jesus belongs to Mary; and she surrenders it.

It is her hour as it is the hour of Jesus. The handmaid of the Lord continues in her service even to martyrdom. She who was not present on Tabor stands close to the Cross; she who had stood aloof from the procession of palms runs eagerly to the altar. The heroine of the "Stabat Mater," the "Mother of Sorrows," will be not merely a saintly Niobe. She is the new Eve, she who together with her Maker recreates the human race, and redeems the souls of men by giving them her Son.

[264]John 10:18.

At the Cross her station keeping,
Stood the mournful mother weeping,
Close to Jesus to the last.

∞

But boundless as is the grief of Mary, is it not allayed by an inner feeling which brings an unspeakable consolation? We must believe that it is so, if it is true that Mary is fully united with Jesus and consecrated to His work. Who shall guide us in these mysteries beyond human comprehension?

We shall see that Jesus has His inner Heaven, even during the Passion. This is not true of Mary, for His was a privilege belonging to Him by virtue of His status as Son of God. But in surmising this Heaven of His does she not make it a little of her own? Nothing of Jesus is alien to her; her heart is united with these secret transports which in Jesus Christ are unfathomable depths.

Similarly, although the future is constrained by the plan of redemption to respect their present grief, yet this future is known to both of them. Behind the Cross they see the fruits of the Cross and its glories, and is this not a mystery of joy to alleviate a mystery of grief?

Reading within the soul of her Son, Mary sees deeper than the Passion and discovers a zone of light. Her tears are prophetic; God who put them into her heart also put there His knowledge of the morrow. She knows; she waits; and her suffering in Jesus is tempered by hope.

Jesus said to the Twelve, "Your sorrow shall be turned into joy."[265] How much more would He say this to His mother! When her sorrows are over, the universe awaits Mary with a tremendous

[265] John 16:20.

acclamation. If the *Magnificat* now gives place to the *Stabat*, this in turn will swell into a greater *Magnificat* still, to which the whole world will lend its joyous voice.

The Almighty who has wrought great things in Mary, will, by her, work still greater. "Fair as the moon, bright as the sun, terrible as an army set forth in battle array,"[266] she with her Son will change the destiny of nations, and Calvary will be to her a memory of something that is past.

We must think of her, then, as mourning and at the same time as in an ecstasy which far outspans the sorrows of the moment; she is as though in a dream. Realities are sometimes so sharp as to force the soul to go beyond them. But Mary's dream is no hallucination peopled by phantoms. It is the dream of creation — or rather, it is that divine dream refashioned and refurbished after man's sin: the dream of redemption.

And now one feature of that destiny is about to be revealed.

Jesus has just lowered His gaze to the group clustered about the Cross. He sees His mother; He sees John, possibly at that moment making some filial gesture toward her. Moved by His deep affection for these two human beings and for those others of whom they are for Him a living symbol, He associates them in one of those rare interruptions of His silence known as the "Seven Words from the Cross."[267]

---

[266] Song of Sol. 6:9.

[267] The traditional seven words from the Cross are "Father, forgive them; for they know not what they do" (Luke 23:34); "Today thou shalt be with me in Paradise" (Luke 23:43); "Woman, behold thy son! . . . Behold thy mother" (John 19:26); "*Eli, Eli, lama sabachthani!* That is to say, 'My God, my God, why hast Thou forsaken me?'" (Matt. 27:46; Mark 15:34); "I thirst" (John 19:28); "It is consummated" (John 19:30); and "Father, into Thy hands I commend my spirit" (Luke 23:46).

He seems to suppress His emotion; He speaks gravely. He does not call Mary His mother, for fear of breaking her heart, but using the solemn and almost impersonal formula which indicates her official function, He says, "Woman, behold thy son," and to John, "Behold thy mother."[268]

The Church has always understood that here John stands as the representative of all men. Mary is entrusted to him personally, and Mary personally adopts him. He is a close relative of Jesus, and Jesus, the model of sons, substitutes him for Himself. But the bond thus created is also a symbol. Mary receives from her Son the whole human race to guard and cherish as her children; the human race receives Mary as its heritage. This tender and touching farewell of Jesus contains a final mystery of love.

∞

This is not the moment to say all that is implied in this multiple gift. Let us remember only that if for us it is a most tender and precious privilege, for Mary it is a more explicit and evident association with Jesus as Redeemer. Jesus asks His mother to adopt His "brethren"; she is to look now not only toward the Cross and toward the tomb, nor even toward the place of ascension and glory, but toward the stage on which the great work is to be played out, a work that calls for her tender and powerful cooperation.

Mary consents; Mary accepts her office. She has no need to rend herself in two, no need to renounce her tears and leave alone in His grief the Son from whom she has received her legacy. It is in Him that she sees all things. Once more she plunges into that gulf of her love that contains all mysteries. She takes Jesus as He

---

[268] John 19:26-27.

is, both in His person and in His function. The new Eve is united to the new Adam, whether it be on the bed of sorrow, or in the generations in which their posterity will live.

His will and testament made, Jesus relapses into His silence, and Mary into her meditation. She cannot protest, she cannot say "No"; nor, without anguish, can she say "Yes." The substitution of a man for her divine Son, of a multitude for the Only-begotten — is this matter for rejoicing? The present has not the right to hide the future from her; still less has the future the right to snatch her from the present. What else can she do save stand erect, body and soul, as ever the submissive handmaid of the Lord?

> At the Cross her station keeping,
> Stood the mournful mother weeping. . . .

∞

At Gibeon in the time of David the tragic Rizpah kept vigil by the gibbet upon which two of her innocent sons were expiating the crime of the people. It was in the early barley harvest, a little later in the year than the Passion of Jesus. And Rizpah took haircloth and spread it upon the rock; she made it her domain, and she would not suffer the birds of the air to devour her children.[269]

The Rizpah of Calvary has not the same freedom. She cannot keep the vultures at bay, and she allows hate to rend the body of her Son. No, she takes her part, not, indeed, in the crime, but in the merciful design of the Father, the Son, and the Holy Spirit.

Spouse of the creative Spirit who renovates the nature of man, mother of the Son, the new Man, and daughter of the Father from whom all things are, Mary assists the family into which her

[269] 2 Kings 21:10 (RSV = 2 Sam. 21:10).

superhuman vocation has assumed her. She is doing a divine work. She is God's helper, and we may believe that when the dying Savior yields up His last thought together with His soul, she will be moved by the Spirit to say with Him, "Father, into Thy hands I commend my Son."

8

His Enemies

After the friends of Jesus have paraded before the eyes of the Crucified and before ours, it is now the turn of His enemies. These are of long standing. Yet their antagonism to Jesus reaches its extreme tension in the end, and the Passion is simply the final stage in a long moral crisis, the explosion provoked by two interacting fluids. Here are the enemies — if we may so judge — in ascending order of guilt: the soldiers, the crowd, Pilate and Herod, the Jewish leaders, Judas.

The soldiers whom we meet in the Passion are Roman soldiers; not the *equites* of the glorious Roman legions, but mercenaries, probably drawn from the neighboring country and therefore, perhaps, not entirely free from Jewish hostility to Jesus. The governor had his cohort, which guarded his person and assisted at his tribunal. The Antonia was a fortress and the presence of the procurator[270] made it the site of the praetorium; this included a

---

[270] An office in the Roman imperial civil service (sometimes charged with the government of minor provinces) in which the official exercised

garrison, a bodyguard, and other henchmen whose duty it was to execute sentence.

But these people, whose behavior will be so savage and inhuman, are not in any degree responsible for the Passion. They are obeying orders; they think they are doing no wrong in carrying out a sentence passed jointly by the Jewish authority and by that of Rome. These two powers assume all responsibility — the external execution of their commands might be regarded as nothing more than an innocent cooperation.

Our Savior's words of pardon, "Father, forgive them, for they know not what they do,"[271] seem to have been designed primarily to excuse His executioners, although we must undoubtedly extend their meaning also to others. In this case, insofar as the soldiers alone are concerned, the verdict pronounced from the Cross would be an exact pronouncement of justice. Pardon is asked for them: therefore they are guilty. But it is said that they do not know what they are doing: therefore, their guilt relates not to what they are doing, but to the manner in which they are doing it.

The fault of these wretches is in the enthusiasm with which they execute the criminal plan of the Jewish leaders, in the base cruelty and barbarous insolence by which they add their own excess to the crime of others. They first stand in need of the sublime forgiveness.

When Jesus looks at these men, and when He beholds the Antonia some four hundred yards to His left, can He forget what He has suffered within the shadow of those cruel ramparts? The scourging is only three hours old, and it still scorches His flesh. It was just now renewed when the garments, still adhering to His

full civil and criminal jurisdiction. Pontius Pilate was procurator of the Roman province of Judea from A.D. 26 to 36.

[271] Luke 23:34.

wounds, were torn from His person. There is reason to think that it took place under conditions more cruel than the law demanded; and why, if not because the human brute thirsts for blood, and these men have unleashed the brute within themselves?

Did it not content their fiendish passion to have scourged the condemned man until He could feel no more? Fine thongs that cut and saw and tear; iron chains loaded with metal that bruise and lay open the flesh; sharp points that pierce and cut to the bone: such is the torture which the wise Roman law reserves for slaves, as a preliminary to the most frightful death devised by man, a death whose stages constituted a refined gradation of torments.

Was this not enough, this anticipated extension of a cruel martyrdom, this calculated infliction of the maximum of savagery? But the soldiers find a means of improving upon it. To the pain which one might have called necessary they find something to add, and so implacable is their brutality that they still have the courage to mock their panting victim.

The scene in the guardroom is even now present before His eyes. Jesus sees it once more and tastes all its bitterness again in the midst of His death agony; and this scene is due entirely to the hirelings of Pilate.

Jesus has been scourged, probably, in the open air, on the *lithostratos* (or "pavement"), before the tribunal[272] — at any rate, in an outer hall.[273] While He is supposed to be replacing His garments the execution squad seizes Him and leads Him to the praetorium, in this case an inner courtyard, where the whole cohort is assembled to watch the fun.

He calls himself a king. Very well, they will adorn Him with the royal emblems. One of them takes off his cloak and throws it

[272] The civil court rostrum or judge's bench in cities of the Roman empire.
[273] John 19:13.

upon the bleeding shoulders: that will do for His purple garment. They see a branch of thorns in the bushes, which they twist into the semblance of a diadem. And it may be, as Calmet suggests, that the thorns were flowering at this time of the year, so that it looks like a garland: and there is the king, joyful and glorious. A reed will do for a scepter, and it is thrust into the manacled fingers, or received passively in His right hand.

Then they roar with laughter, and they strike Him. The crown, which they have placed lightly upon His head for fear of pricking themselves, is now driven in as they smite Him with reeds. They rain blows upon this mock potentate who makes no attempt to defend Himself. They spit in His face and, filing before Him, they vie with each other in inventing an original jeer, a new variation of their cruel theme. "They came to Him, and said: Hail, king of the Jews!"[274] "And bowing their knees, they adored Him,"[275] adding spice to their ironical homage with their spittle and blows.

It has been suggested that these mock courts were part of the ordinary routine; examples are cited in Persia and even in the Holy Land itself. Some have even thought that it was a ritual. At the very best this would be an attenuating circumstance. It remains true that this barbarous proceeding is one of the most revolting scenes of the Passion.

When the final torment of the Cross is reached it is needless for the soldiers to invent new horrors; it has an atrocity all its own. But mockery will still have its say: "And the soldiers also mocked Him, . . . saying: If thou be the king of the Jews, save thyself!"[276]

It is this idea of kingship that seems especially to have appealed to these poor wretches. They see in Jesus nothing more than a

[274]John 19:3.
[275]Mark 15:19.
[276]Luke 23:36-37.

fallen pretender, a comrade who has tried to step out of the ranks, and whom they are very glad to put back in his place. The mob has these sentiments; it is obsessed by the idea of equality on a low level. "He that exalteth himself shall be humbled":[277] the mob has its own way of applying this principle.

There is nothing that these brutes do not turn into a mockery, even the alleviation that they grant Him when they offer Him to drink. They seem to say to Him, "Do you need to be comforted, you, the king of the Jews? Why not use your power for this, too?"

Let us notice, however, that their derision does not seem here to exclude all sentiment of humanity. But their mockery spoils it and by its very triviality offends our feelings of reverence.

The torment of thirst was one of the worst that the crucified had to undergo, and the soldiers knew it. They had drink ready at hand. In the East the jug is always a necessary article if you are staying long in one place. The stay on Calvary was likely to be a prolonged one, and moreover the weather was close. St. John tells us that there was "a vessel set there, full of vinegar,"[278] that is acidulated water, the Roman *posca*; and the mouth of the vessel was doubtless stopped by the sponge which they will use to give drink to the Sufferer.

When the Savior avows His distress, seeming to ask for relief with the words "I thirst,"[279] the soldiers do not refuse to share their drink with Him. But at the same time it strikes them as funny: "We are giving the king of the Jews a drink!" And they chuckle as though it were a timely jest.

A further incident increases their merriment. Jesus has just uttered the tragic cry "My God, my God, why hast Thou forsaken

[277] Matt. 23:12; Luke 14:11, 18:14.
[278] John 19:29.
[279] John 19:28.

me?" which in Aramaic is *Eli, Eli, lamma sabachtani?*[280] Now the Jews who are present know these words perfectly well, for they are the opening verse of the twenty-first Psalm;[281] but they pretend to think that Jesus is calling upon Elijah.[282] They cannot be really mistaken because Elijah is *Eliah,* not *Eli* or *Eloi;* they are making a pun which to them seems apposite. Elijah, according to the belief of the Jews, was to be the precursor of the Messiah, and those who credited the latter with poor and modest beginnings believed that Elijah would come to raise him up and manifest his glory. So it was a fine irony to say, "Hear this Messiah in distress calling for the help of Elijah; Elijah is sure to come!"

And so the soldiers hearing this, and perhaps being natives and understanding the reference, enter into the joke, and when one of their number takes the sponge soaked in the *posca,* and sets it upon a reed to reach up to the burning lips, they call to him, "Let us see whether Elijah will come to deliver him!"[283]

And the soldier, as though taking up the refrain, but lending it another shade of meaning, answers, "Stay, let us see if Elijah comes to take him down!"[284] as though to say, "We must give Elijah time to come, and so we must help the sufferer to last a little longer."

One would like to suppose that it is human respect or necessity that makes the soldier speak in this way, that in reality he is stirred by pity and is trying to force the hand of his comrades. Two of the evangelists represent him as "running" to fulfill his office;[285] and it is only zeal that runs, while irony seeks to prolong the torture. If

[280] Matt. 27:46; Mark 15:34.
[281] Ps. 21:1 (RSV = Ps. 22:1).
[282] Matt. 27:47; Mark 15:35.
[283] Matt. 27:49.
[284] Mark 15:36.
[285] Matt. 27:48; Mark 15:36.

this soldier was a timid sort of Good Thief, or at the worst a good fellow moved to compassion by so much suffering, it would explain why the gentle Savior welcomed his kind service. Jesus, who is ready to appreciate even the minutest particle of goodness, drinks from the sponge with a sort of joy, which itself is a reward.

∞

The last action of the soldiers before the Savior's death is the sharing of the garments. This is no new outrage; it was a recognized perquisite. A rescript of Hadrian[286] some years later regulated the practice by ordaining that the legitimate spoils were to consist only of the garments of the condemned man together with the small objects and pocket money which he had upon him at the moment of his arrest, but not precious jewels or a well-filled girdle.

One shudders at the thought that such louts are to wear the garments which have clothed the adorable Body; the desecration revolts us. But these wretched soldiers cannot be held responsible; in this, as in all else, "they know not what they do."[287]

∞

These words from the Cross which keep recurring to our minds seem to express to perfection what the Crucified felt in regard to His executioners. He does not curse them; in His sight they are the instruments of His Passion, like the hammers, the nails, and the ropes, save that they have a soul, which He loves.

Without exonerating them, the sacred necessity of His death shelters His executioners in His eyes. He sees them as protected

[286]Roman emperor (A.D. 117-138).
[287]Luke 23:34.

155

under "the will of the Father."[288] He would almost thank them for "lifting Him up from the earth" that He may "draw all things to Himself."[289] And as for what is due to their own initiative, the incidents in the guardroom of the Antonia, is He not grateful to them for giving the world — better even than did Veronica — a picture which it will never forget?

Ecce Homo! "Behold the man!"[290] To whom do we owe this picture of the man who is God and our brother, this embodiment of meritorious grief, of kingship vanquished by love? Surely it was the angel of the Passion rather than a band of mercenaries that designed this noble figure! The piety of generations has engraved it upon men's souls. Art, even profane art, never tires of contemplating and glorifying it, and the day will come when the impression of sublimity will become so strong as to make its horror disappear.

The mob on Calvary is not entirely hostile; but we are concerned here only with the hostile section. And this now predominates, as it always does when once it has assumed numerical importance and its leaders have issued the order of the day.

The incredible thing is that it should have been found possible to mobilize against Jesus so many people who for various reasons ought to have been His friends. They had received from Him nothing but benefits. His words had awakened their slumbering hearts; His goodness had won their affection; His miracles had aroused their admiration; His condemnation of abuses could not

[288]John 6:40.
[289]John 12:32.
[290]John 19:5.

but command their sympathy; and His promises of happiness, even if they were not believed, must at least have flattered their dreams.

What is their grievance? That the leaders of the Jews should have hated Jesus is perhaps intelligible, but the enmity of the crowd is most mysterious. It is only at the last moment that it becomes manifest, and then only under the stimulus of encouragement from the priests.

At the beginning of His sacred ministry Jesus had applied to Himself the words of the prophet: "The spirit of the Lord is upon me, wherefore He hath anointed me to preach the gospel to the poor. He hath sent me to heal the contrite of heart, to preach deliverance to the captives, and sight to the blind, to set at liberty them that are bruised, to preach the acceptable year of the Lord, and the day of reward."[291]

This program had aroused intense enthusiasm. It is true that there was annoyance at some of His reproaches, and that among His own people Jesus had already experienced something of the fickle moods of mankind. Still, on the whole He had been well received by the masses.

If Jesus complained of their tepidity and their incredulity, of their selfishness and their demands, He did not attribute hostile sentiments to His hearers. Often He had been acclaimed; they had wanted to make Him king. He was received and welcomed with gratitude, and during these last few days since the raising of Lazarus, their love for Him seemed to have reached its zenith.

"A great prophet has arisen in the midst of us! God has visited His people! He has done all things well! Never has man spoken as this man! He is Elijah! He is John the Baptist risen again, or one of the prophets! He is the Messiah: Hosanna to the son of David!

[291] Luke 4:18-19; Cf. Isa. 61:1-2.

Blessed is he that cometh in the name of the Lord!" Such were the cries that saluted Him.

Even during the Passion itself, at Pilate's house, the crowd does not seem ill disposed at first. The leaders had not summoned them; it was hardly likely! Had it not been for Judas and the opportunity he offered, they would willingly have postponed the satisfaction of their hate to avoid this concourse. "Not on the festival day," they said, "lest there be a tumult among the people."[292]

The crowd has assembled for reasons of its own. They have a right to have a prisoner released to them on this day, and they are going to claim that right. Perhaps they are thinking of Barabbas, perhaps of Jesus, who is just at this moment appearing before the tribunal.[293]

Unhappily for the popular choice or for its constancy, the leaders take a hand; they have time to do so, for this is the interval during which the procurator's wife interrupts the proceedings. The mutual explanations of the pair must have taken a moment or two, and it was natural that a certain time should be allowed to the claimants to decide upon their choice.

Pilate has just given them the option: "Which of the two will you that I release unto you?" And he has shown them in which direction his own inclination lies: "Will you that I release unto you the king of the Jews?"[294] Left to themselves, those in the crowd might answer in the affirmative, but the leaders are rousing them now; their high priests have control over them, in spite of their complaints. Moreover, Pilate has irritated them by twice referring jocularly to "their king."[295]

[292] Matt. 26:5.
[293] Mark 15:11-13.
[294] Mark 15:9.
[295] Mark 15:9, 12.

King, king, always this king! And a broken-down king at that! He arouses their derision more than their pity: a Messiah in chains before a Roman governor! This seems to be the kernel of the matter in the eyes of these Israelites, who yesterday were enthusiastic, a few moments ago were in doubt, and now are suddenly hostile and furious.

Mobs do not like to be disillusioned; and the man who disappoints them may pass in a moment from the rank of a national hero to nothing, and even to less than nothing. The sympathies of the mob are liable to revulsions. Many a crashing fall in history has been due to no more than this.

Think what a disillusionment it is for the Jews to see Jesus in this condition before Pilate, to say nothing of the other accusations against Him to which that condition easily lent credit. The Liberator of the chosen people appearing as a leader of sedition before a Roman tribunal and unable to acquit himself of the charge! This is the Pauline "scandal of the Cross"[296] by anticipation, and we can understand that an infuriated crowd will leave Him to His fate.

From disappointment they pass to spite, from spite to anger, and under the ceaseless encouragement of their iniquitous leaders they are easily roused to exasperation. The word *cross* has been spoken; it is taken up and repeated. The penalty of crucifixion has been so often inflicted on Jews that they are surprised at the hesitation of the governor. Once they have rejected Jesus, He is nothing more nor less for them than an agitator and an enemy of the empire. "What will you that I do with Him?" asks Pilate. "What you have done to so many others," they answer in reply, "Crucify Him!"[297]

[296] Cf. 1 Cor. 1:23.
[297] Matt. 27:22; Mark 15:13; Luke 23:20-21; John 19:15.

Once the change of feeling is thus achieved, the taste of blood now begins to intoxicate the mob; a thrill of cruelty runs through them all. To any further questions or objections the maddened crowd has only one reply, given with increasing violence: "Crucify Him! Crucify Him!" And it does not stop there; it involves the whole people in its own responsibility, and not only the present generation but posterity as well: "His blood be upon us and upon our children!"[298]

And that prayer will be answered. But what a tragedy for Him who would have gathered this thankless people "as the hen gathers her chickens under her wings!"[299] He has come to them with a message of happiness, and they hate Him and blaspheme. If that message was only a dream it was at any rate a dream of goodness; and their only answer is the nightmare of death.

This people, which has awaited and expected Him for so many centuries, receives Him and fails to know Him for what He is. He who was to come is come, and He departs carrying all His blessings with Him. His nation scorns Him, kills Him, drives Him forth; even dead they will have Him only outside their walls. And while He dies they scoff and sneer. Even those who have not come to see Him die are over there on the terraces of their houses, waving their arms and crying out like madmen. And Jesus, whose Cross raises Him above the level of the walls, can see these traitors to His love, these distant enemies.

As the procession passed the Gate of Ephraim, those who had been waiting there since the great news came from the praetorium, who had heard the legal formula "Go, *lictor*, prepare the cross!" pronounced,[300] must have broken forth again into tumultuous fury.

[298] Matt. 27:25.

[299] Matt. 23:37; Luke 13:34.

[300] A *lictor* was a Roman officer whose duties included attendance upon

For now it was their fury that they showed, not their desires or their requests. The cruel gaiety of this day had gone to everybody's head; the word *cross* was on the lips of them all, and the word *blood* and the word *death*, mingling with *Galilean, rabbi, prophet, Messiah*; and every word was uttered with a sneer.

Every savage instinct latent in the heart of man was awake; souls frothed over with rage, and this anticipatory delegation of those who in every generation would hate and oppose Christ, vented itself in a cry of satanic joy.

The darkness and the other portents that are soon to appear will damp this delirious frenzy. A thrill of fear will pass through the city; hearts will be heavy; those who now acclaim the death of the Savior will beat their breasts. Once more the fickle crowd will change, in its emotional and childish fashion. Yet the problem still remains: how did this transformation which we have described become possible? General explanations do not satisfy the mind; is there not one which perhaps goes deep to the heart of things?

∞

The mystics tell us that a great moral lapse is always preceded by hidden causes. Men fall because they are imperfect; the occasion only contributes the stumbling block. In this case the imperfection consisted in the fact that the Jewish masses at that time were prone to mystical curiosity and superstitious practices.

The success which Jesus achieved among the masses was due to the interest of the moment and the enthusiasm aroused by His miracles, to the fascination of His discourse, to the sardonic

chief magistrates appearing in public, clearing the way for them and ensuring that proper respect was given to them. Lictors were also charged with the apprehension and punishment of criminals.

satisfaction of hearing their leaders criticized and of seeing them defied, as well as to the impetuosity of an imagination captivated by its own dreams, rather than to a fully convinced adherence to Him and His teaching.

This people had been dazzled, not convinced; and its carnal expectations were disappointed without becoming adapted to the ideal which took their place. Jesus as a political Messiah, a favorer of external pomp, a dispenser of tangible and manifest benefits, such as the casting off of the Roman yoke, the abolition of tithes and the return of the Jews of the dispersal — this is what would have won over these "stiff-necked"[301] tribes.

But the aims and the doctrines of the Savior were not of this kind; and this is the reason why, as soon as they see their selfish hopes disappointed, the crowd turns against Him. Their favor becomes hostility.

What Jesus fails to give He seems to snatch from their grasp, and the Messiah of their dreams appears as the victim of this Messiah who is made ridiculous. Jesus finds Himself crowned with thorns and given a mock scepter because one day He refused to let them make Him king.

∞

Let us not in these days be too hard on a mob which was so fickle and finally so cruel. For it is to them that we owe these last days of Jesus. True, they acclaimed His death, and if it wasn't for them perhaps Pilate would not have given way to the Sanhedrin. But this last point is not certain, and on the other hand it is certain that if the enthusiasm of Palm Sunday and the earlier popularity

---

[301] Exod. 33:3; Acts 7:51.

had not formed a bulwark around the Teacher, Jesus would soon have fallen a victim to His task.

How many times might His career otherwise have been cut short! The traps that had been set for Him failed because He had the sympathy and the support of His audience. His reputation was His safeguard. If the crowds had remained silent, would His most convincing repartees have carried the day?

And when He ventured to drive the sellers out of the Temple, would they have been content merely to ask, "By what authority dost thou these things?"[302] — if He had not been supported by the crowd? One did not touch the Temple with impunity, even to purify it. Still less, without the risk of death, could one interfere with sacrosanct reputations and with privileges from which the whole of the ruling caste derived its profits.

However, in this as in other agencies which operate in the Passion, not everything is left to the free play of human wills, be they friendly or hostile. The mob — like the soldiers — is not primarily responsible for the death of Jesus. Men's actions are their own, and they will answer for them; but by means of men and their actions God governs the universe.

All that happens on Calvary happens in obedience to God's will. This disorder is God's design; this hate is God's love. In the course of centuries during which the effects of the Passion are worked out, the conflict of minds and the clash of wills are but the reflection of an immutable order.

The designs of eternity are accomplished, and in the eyes of Jesus, as in the eyes of those of us who contemplate it, the tumult of the masses at the Gate of Ephraim, like the tumult of the ages, is the tumult of God.

---

[302] Matt. 21:23; Mark 11:28; Luke 20:2.

∞

From His Cross Jesus cannot see Pilate or Herod; He sees only their dwellings, the Antonia with its five towers and, to the southwest of the gibbet, the palace of the Hasmonaeans.[303]

Jesus had always despised Herod, the incestuous tetrarch who slew John the Baptist; He called him "that fox," and defied him to put an end to His work before the moment which He Himself had decreed.[304]

When Pilate sends Jesus to this vile monarch in order to extricate himself from a difficult situation, Herod does not appear to be harsh with Him or indeed to have any recollection of his own plans in the Savior's regard; he was so frivolous! He is pleased to see Jesus. He is even "very glad; for he was desirous of a long time to see Him, because he had heard many things of Him."[305]

Nonetheless Herod has summoned his guard — perhaps because he is a little in fear of some mysterious power, perhaps because he wants his soldiers to share an interesting spectacle. At any rate he expects to see "some sign."[306] He wants an amusing prisoner, just as the mob wants a glorious Messiah. In this he is like one of the mob, and also in the fact that he is talkative: he proceeds to question him "with many words."[307]

But Jesus holds His peace.

Oh, that silence! How overwhelming and how galling for the insolent tyrant, and how instructive for us! Since Herod has no

---

[303] A Jewish family that included the Maccabees, as well as the high priests and kings who ruled Judea from 142 to 63 B.C.

[304] Luke 13:32.

[305] Luke 23:8.

[306] Ibid.

[307] Luke 23:9.

religious authority, Jesus has no reason to explain His mission. The truth would be of no use to Herod because he is not sincere. A miracle would be a mere bribe, and would be to tempt God. Jesus shuts Himself up in His silence; He is humbly and patiently resigned, but He does not commit Himself.

And now Herod, for the second time scorned, scorns Jesus in return. Without doubt he hates Him secretly — a tiger lurks behind that frivolous demeanor. But he hides his wrath. He shows only his disdain, and thinking to make a witty end to the interview, he sends the pretender away clothed in a gorgeous robe, a festive garment such as princes wear for their investiture.

The Gospel tells us that Pilate and Herod were at that time on unfriendly terms. Jesus, as a Galilean, was subject to the jurisdiction of Herod, but having been arrested in Judea He was at Pilate's disposition. Hence the governor in sending Him to the tetrarch of Galilee was not only getting rid of an awkward prisoner but also paying a friendly compliment to Herod. Herod is flattered, and replies with a gesture of declining the honor. He passes judgment after a manner, and at the same time returns the compliment. And this is the reason, so the Gospel remarks, why they become friends from that day forth.[308]

Friends like to joke with each other. But Herod is not to be taken in by a thing like that. He knows what to think of the "kingship" of this poor misguided man! He is a plaything with which they can amuse themselves while Pilate, the experienced politician, makes up his mind what to do with him. He may do what he likes!

And so the Savior of the world becomes the sport of frivolous princes, while the fury of the mob roars an accompaniment.

---

[308]Luke 23:12.

∽

Pilate's part in the affair is more important than that of the tetrarch; and so he holds a more prominent place in our thoughts, as he does in those of Jesus. Yet Jesus speaks of him with indulgence. This Roman also has a providential part to play. "Thou shouldst not have any power against me," the Savior tells him, "unless it were given thee from above."[309] Pascal makes the following reflection concerning this: "Jesus would not be killed without the forms of justice; for it is more ignominious to die at the hands of justice than at the hands of an unruly mob."

∽

Two sentences have already been passed, but neither of them is a sentence of death. And everything must be done according to the law, so that it may be said that Jesus is guilty, so that He may be treated as guilty, for the purpose of the merciful substitution by which He is to save the souls of men.

However, in the temporal order of the divine plan each man has his own responsibility, and the Savior does not absolve Pilate from blame; He says only that his guilt is not so great as another guilt, a guilt which stands alone — that of Judas.[310]

∽

We must do Pilate the justice of recognizing that he saw clearly through the game of the Sanhedrin. Their first words betrayed them. When he asks them, "What accusation do you bring against

[309] John 19:11.

[310] Ibid.: "He that hath delivered me to thee, hath the greater sin."

this man?" they answer with a lofty impatience which is suspicious in the circumstances: "If he were not a malefactor, we would not have delivered him up to you."[311] They had hoped for a merely formal confirmation of their sentence.

Understanding the situation, Pilate now maneuvers in order to free the prisoner. But his sentiment of justice has no very deep roots; violence and obstinacy will soon overcome it. This politician who would like to do the right thing, is not one of those who will expose themselves to ruin or risk for justice's sake. He is in favor of justice when it costs nothing. He is ready for any compromise which his peace or his credit with the Emperor may demand. And that is his crime.

A comparison of the accounts found in the Gospels gives us a fair idea of what takes place. The Sanhedrin, called upon for an explanation, brings three charges against Jesus: He is a disturber of the peace; He forbids the payment of tribute; He says that He is Christ the King. Pilate, good lawyer and businesslike Roman that he is, goes straight to the root of the matter. He considers only the last accusation, on which the others depend.

He questions Jesus, and the answers which he receives convince him that His is a mystical kingship from which the state has nothing to fear, and in which a political judge has no business to meddle. He declares that so far as he can see the man is innocent. To strengthen his position he tries to make Jesus speak before these leaders of His countrymen, to reduce the latter to confusion and to lay bare the sentiments by which they are animated.

Jesus does not say a word, and Pilate is amazed, because he is offering Him a chance at His life. But Jesus has already accepted death; He has no intention of defending Himself. His task is

[311] John 18:29-30.

accomplished and awaits only the final seal. The idea of discussing Jewish questions with this foreigner is repugnant to Him. He has said enough to enlighten an upright conscience and to enable it to avoid passing an unjust sentence. In His opinion that is enough, and henceforth He remains silent.

Pilate then begins to admire Jesus. Few accused men hold life so cheaply; and none has ever assumed an attitude so noble. Pilate would like to save this "just man,"[312] as his centurion will call Him later, and as he himself calls Him soon. But he wants to save Him without giving any cause for complaint against himself and without making himself vulnerable to accusations before the tribunal of Caesar.

He addresses the crowd. He has realized that the keynote of the discussion is here, that the "envy"[313] of the Sanhedrin is directed against the popularity of Jesus and the diffusion of ideas which threaten their own influence. It is a good move, because it will be difficult for the accusers to admit their real sentiments and to oppose the people's desires.

But if the move were to be successful, he should not speak to them in such a way as to alienate their sympathies; and this is exactly what Pilate does, in his irrepressible scorn for this Jewish rabble. "Will you that I deliver to you the king of the Jews?"[314] "What shall I do with your king?"[315] "Shall I crucify your king?"[316] All this is said with scornful intent, and he is wrong if he thinks that they do not see it. An appeal to their good feeling might have saved all; irony will only precipitate the crisis.

[312] Luke 23:47.
[313] Matt. 27:18.
[314] Mark 15:9.
[315] Cf. Mark 15:12.
[316] John 19:15.

Meanwhile the high priests have not been wasting their time. During the intervals of the discussion and the questionings, and while Pilate and his wife are talking about a dream, they have been working on the passions of the crowd. They have aroused their vanity. They have accused Jesus of a thousand misdeeds, and when the governor insistently asks them, "What evil hath he done?"[317] nobody is in the mood for argument. Hate is given full rein and the torrent rushes forth.

The sending of the prisoner to Herod has not improved matters. On the contrary, it has allowed further time for the passions of the crowd to be inflamed. Nor is it of any use to suggest a lesser penalty. These concessions merely ruin the last chances, for they show audacity that it has won the day.

When the scourging has taken place — and this already meant that Jesus was abandoned, for according to the law it was the usual preliminary to the capital penalty — Pilate makes a final attempt to negotiate with the crowd in an effort to avoid the supreme crime. He notes what his soldiers have done in the guardroom and the state to which they have reduced the prisoner. He does not blame them; no doubt it was quite natural, and it may serve his purpose. "Behold the man!" he says; "behold your king!"[318] But it is too late; it is a mistake to show blood to a tiger. The mob is beyond control. It roars; it appeals to Caesar.[319]

And that is the end; the word *Caesar* is all-powerful, and stronger than a conscience such as Pilate's. Henceforth Jesus has everything against Him, save justice. And justice has not enough power over a weak, ambitious, carefree dilettante to make him defy a coalition which has now become a menace.

[317] Mark 15:14.
[318] John 19:5, 14.
[319] John 19:15.

Pilate "gave sentence that it should be as they required."[320] Instead of being a judge he becomes an executioner. He, who is responsible, abdicates his judgeship and becomes an accomplice in crime, and he thinks to shield himself by washing his hands, saying as he does so, "I am innocent of the blood of this just man. Look you to it."[321]

His cowardly maneuver is partially successful. The crowd, in the name of the people, takes upon itself and upon its children responsibility for the crime. But in taking it upon itself it only shares it; it cannot exonerate the judge without whom nothing could have been done.

As for the washing of hands, that is mere superstitious mumbo-jumbo. The Romans and the Jews, with some slight differences of interpretation, used this gesture to ward off the vendetta. Pilate believes in this sort of conjuring; cowardice and superstition usually go hand in hand. Besides, his wife will be comforted. He does not follow her advice, but he gives her some semblance of satisfaction: "You see, I am free of this matter, and the people have taken all the blame!"

Let us not enlarge upon the vileness of such conduct nor upon the heavy sentence which the Judge of Calvary ought in justice to pass upon it. His verdict in fact is a most merciful one. But mercy presupposes a sin, and this sin is so frightful that its horror can only be diminished by the comparison which Jesus makes with another: "He that hath delivered me to thee hath the greater sin."[322]

[320]Luke 23:24.
[321]Matt. 27:24.
[322]John 19:11.

∞

Before considering this supreme responsibility and before mentioning Judas, we must consider the case of the Sanhedrin and its unofficial accomplices, the Sadducees and Pharisees.

These Jesus can see. They are come to gloat over His sufferings, and with their own eyes to satisfy themselves of the success of their machinations. Their self-respect does not forbid them to mingle with the mob, with the flunkeys and the rude soldiery, to insult their dying victim.

To what lengths can men be led by passion! Is this the place for these high dignitaries who think themselves so magnificent? Have they no fear of losing their influence by betraying their baseness? Has death no seriousness for them?

Yet there is something in their attitude that marks them out from the rest. These jeerers do not address Jesus directly; the mockeries that are meant for Him they trade among themselves.

They have no need to indulge in direct discourse with Jesus; others are seeing to that, others whose tongues they themselves have primed with insults. The passersby, the onlookers, the soldiers, and the robbers are only their representatives. From time to time the leaders mingle with the group which they have organized;[323] but it is chiefly from one to another, in a select company, that they pass their stream of hate.

"In like manner also the chief priests, mocking, said with the scribes one to another: He saved others; himself he cannot save. Let Christ the king of Israel come down now from the cross, that we may see and believe."[324] One might almost say that they are trying to give one another courage, each of them striving to prove

[323] Luke 23:35.
[324] Mark 15:31-32.

himself in the right and to demonstrate it to others: a system of collective reassurance.

It is possible that some of them are a little doubtful and regret the step they have taken. We know that the council was not unanimous and that Joseph of Arimathea "had not consented to their counsel and doings."[325] It would be well to have a final confirmation of their verdict.

After all, there would still be time to revise their decision! They are not prejudiced! Let Christ, with whom all things are possible, come down "now" from the Cross! They will forget that He ever allowed Himself to be nailed to it; they will then acknowledge His power and His kingship. Let them only see that, and they will believe.

It may be noticed that the conversation of these priests includes an avowal. "He saved others." Of course, these words might be understood ironically, as if to say, "He *claims* to have saved others." But the context and previous events suggest rather that their conscience is troubled concerning the "signs" which the divine Master has given in such abundance. They have seen miracles and have shut their eyes. When they were shown the sick who had been healed, the dead who had been raised to life, they said, "Let him show us a sign from Heaven!"[326] As the number of miracles increased they asked for more and kept on saying, "What sign dost thou show?"[327]

Bad faith always acts in this way. Nothing is ever enough; the more you do to satisfy it the more it demands, warding off the inevitable submission by constant postponement. Did not Renan demand that a miracle should be worked before his eyes and in the

[325]Luke 23:51.
[326]Cf. Matt. 16:1.
[327]John 6:30.

presence of a jury of scientists, that it should obey his orders and be repeated as often as he wished? In this way he shut himself out from all possibility of eventual conviction; miracles need cause him no anxiety.

The Sanhedrin anticipates his lesson. Just look at this Messiah! Three nails are too strong for him; and you would have us accept these pretended miracles which, if he were a real Messiah, he might easily confirm with this final and irrefutable proof! "Vah, thou that destroyest the temple of God and in three days does rebuild it; save thy own self. If thou be the Son of God, come down from the cross!"[328] "He trusted in God; let Him now deliver him if He will have him; for he said: I am the Son of God."[329] "Let him save himself, if he be Christ, the elect of God."[330] "If thou be the Christ, save thyself and us."[331]

This last utterance came from one of the crosses, becoming mingled with those that were shrieked by the crowd or murmured by the high priests among themselves. But the origin of them all is the same: a command flung at the Sufferer, accompanied with the wagging of the head, a gesture of sarcasm and cruel enjoyment. For there are two sentiments here: the pride that mocks and the hate that gloats.

∞

Jesus who refused to protest while there was still hope of saving His life will not give answer now that He is nailed to the Cross. These suggestions are not new to Him; He heard them at the

[328] Matt. 27:40.
[329] Matt. 27:43.
[330] Luke 23:35.
[331] Luke 23:39.

beginning of His mission. Satan said to Him, "If thou be the Son of God, cast thyself down."[332] But what purpose would that miracle have served? And what purpose would it serve now if Jesus saved Himself, only to show that He was incapable of saving us?

He will work a miracle that is greater still. For which is the more difficult, to come down from the Cross or to come forth from the sepulcher? For a long time Jesus has referred His enemies to the sign of Jonah the prophet,[333] a miracle so striking in the eyes of the future that the Apostles will consider themselves to have a sufficient mission if it is only to be witnesses of this.

∞

It is instructive to inquire, as Pilate was inquiring just now, into the motive of the conflict between Jesus and the leaders of the Jews which has now led to the Cross. We have said what were the reasons of the crowd. Their leaders share these reasons with them, although their more accurate knowledge and their better education saves them from the grosser errors of the mob. But they have other reasons, and much stronger ones.

To appreciate them we must know what these people are.

The leaders properly so-called composed the Sanhedrin, which is simultaneously tribunal, parliament, and council. This assembly comprises three orders: the "Chief priests," the "Scribes," and the "Ancients." The first of these dignitaries include the high priest of the year, the former high priests, their near relatives, and the heads of the great priestly families. The second, the Scribes, are the body of the learned. The Ancients are any leading priests or laity who do not belong to either of the first two categories.

[332] Matt. 4:6.
[333] Matt. 12:39; Luke 11:29.

The Sanhedrin draws its members in unequal proportions from the two religious sects which divide Israel: that of the Sadducees and that of the Pharisees.

The Pharisees are the "separated," the "pure," zealous for the Law, subtle commentators and casuists, rigorists in their policy at home, defiant to outsiders, and the great enemies of the Roman domination. They expect the Messiah; and they are spiritualists, believing in the angels, the soul, and immortality.

The Sadducees on the contrary, rich and few in number, are more or less sceptics, materialists, and pleasure-seekers. They represent an arrogant aristocracy. They accept the Law but reject the commentaries and all the traditions of the Pharisees. They do not care about the Messiah; they put up with the Roman rule and it is their policy to live on peaceful terms with the foreigner. They are friends of Herod and of Caesar. The people dislike them, while they have a weakness for the Pharisees, being impressed by their outward piety and more exalted doctrines.

The rich man of the parable seems to be one of these Sadducees who, after a life of selfish enjoyment, wakes up suddenly to find himself in another life, in which he had not believed, and for which he was not prepared.

But, sharply divided as all these people are, they can nevertheless unite under the influence of a common interest or a great passion, and this is the case in regard to Jesus.

The Sadducees oppose Jesus for political reasons: He undermines their influence, they say, and puts the whole nation in danger. This is the argument of Caiaphas: "You know nothing. Neither do you consider that it is expedient for you that one man should die for the people, and that the whole nation perish not."[334]

---

[334] John 11:49-50.

They have little interest in doctrinal disputes, except insofar as they may serve their purpose.

It is on this last point that the Pharisees, on the other hand, mainly base their opposition to Jesus; they attack Him in the name of Mosaic doctrine, which in their eyes is compromised by any innovation. They are purists, and Jesus is corrupting the people. They have a tradition to which they are more attached than to the Law itself; Jesus takes no account of their tradition, to which He opposes a true morality.

Jesus does not observe the ceremonial ablutions; He consorts with publicans and sinners; neither He nor His disciples fast; they do not observe the Sabbath, since on that day the Twelve rub the ears of corn as they pass through the fields, and Jesus Himself heals the paralytics.[335] He is a man of Satan, the envoy of Baalzebub, the god of Ekron.[336]

During the whole course of His public life Jesus found Himself confronted by these Pharisees. The least hostile among them could not forgive Him for bringing the message of eternal youth into their antiquated world; the majority of them attacked Him furiously on every count. The Sadducees for the most part watched Him from the background, although from time to time we find them also taking a prominent part.

Certainly Christ did not spare their feelings. His doctrine made no attempt to compromise with their ideas. His practice took no account of their precepts. The opposition which He marked between the old Law and the new could not but arouse their enmity. Nor did they derive any satisfaction from the palliative "I am not come to destroy but to fulfill."[337]

---

[335] Mark 2.
[336] 4 Kings 1:2 (RSV = 2 Kings 1:2).
[337] Matt. 5:17.

Jesus claimed to forgive sins; He gave Himself out as lord of the Sabbath; He allowed Himself to be called Messiah, Son of David, Son of God, and by other "blasphemous" names. But above all — above all, He had on many occasions taken so vigorous an offensive against the leaders of His people, He had overwhelmed them with such scornful invective, that a terrible reaction was only to be expected.

"Take heed," He said, "and beware of the leaven of the Pharisees and Sadducees,"[338] "which is hypocrisy."[339] He described these stiff-necked partisans as pseudopurists rather than whom even courtesans would enter the kingdom of God. He contrasted with their ostentatious prayers that of the publican, who goes away justified while they are condemned. He mocked their posing as professional fasters; He scorned their long flowing robes, their fringes, and their phylacteries. The Ten Commandments danced in little scrolls before their eyes but it did not govern their conduct. Their religion was only a source of profit, an opportunity for "taking the first places."[340] Their love of the Law was a formalism that favored the letter against the spirit, sacrificing the law of God to empty traditions. They had commercialized the kingdom of Heaven; they made themselves its gatekeepers and trafficked in the tickets, but they themselves did not enter in. "Blind leaders of the blind,"[341] they inevitably lead the whole caravan into the pit.

The climax of their hatred and the resolution of the crisis which during these three years has passed through so many phases, are reached two or three days before the Passion. It is at this time that we hear the indictment fulminated in the Temple itself

[338] Matt. 16:6.
[339] Luke 12:1.
[340] Matt. 23:6; Mark 12:39; Luke 20:46.
[341] Matt. 15:14.

against those who claim to be its guardians: "Woe to you, Scribes and Pharisees, hypocrites; because you make clean the outside of the cup and of the dish, but within you are full of rapine and uncleanness. . . . Whited sepulchers, which outwardly appear to men beautiful but within are full of dead men's bones, and of all filthiness. . . . You serpents, generation of vipers, how will you flee from the judgment of Hell?"[342]

These anathemas were followed by a challenge, of which none could fail to see the significance. In the person of His own enemies Jesus recalled all those who in the past had killed the prophets: "You are witnesses against yourselves, that you are the sons of them that killed the prophets. Fill ye up then the measure of your fathers. . . . That upon you may come all the just blood that hath been shed upon the earth, from the blood of Abel the just, even unto the blood of Zechariah the son of Barachiah, whom you killed between the Temple and the altar."[343]

It may well be imagined that such language was a sentence of death for its author. Henceforth, perhaps even before this date, the opposition of the leaders of Israel takes on an official form. A judicial process is set in motion; and this is the reason why the Gospel will now always refer to the Pharisees and Sadducees only under the names of their representatives in the Sanhedrin: the "Chief priests" for the Sadducees, the "Scribes" for the Pharisees, and the "Ancients," who comprise members of both.

The opinion of the first mentioned would weigh most with the Roman authority, because this timeserving aristocracy was favorable to Rome, and because it was in possession of the religious power, although it was obliged, by reason of popular sentiment, to exercise it more or less in dependence upon the Pharisees. Hence

[342] Matt. 23:25, 27, 33.
[343] Matt. 23: 31-32, 35.

it is the chief priests who are in the foreground at Pilate's tribunal, and their hatred is the most furious of all because it is the most sacrilegious and the most bitterly selfish.

Such is the rage that possesses them that no torment seems sufficiently cruel to inflict upon their fallen enemy. These souls of mud and gall are also thirsty for blood. Their visages mask a brutal and passionate hate. For three years they have been fighting for this: their victory must be marked by a nameless punishment.

What is it that they demand? What is it that they urge the mob to ask, in addition to Barabbas, as a present for their feast day?

It is to be feared that in our minds the picture of crucifixion has become somewhat dulled; that our familiarity with the elegant crucifixes of silver and ivory which we see at our bedsides, the bronze crucifixes of the highways, the carved works of art and tiny pendants that we wear, have deadened in us the appreciation of all that was involved in that furious cry, "Crucify Him!"

The penalty of crucifixion was regarded among the Romans as the most cruel and infamous of all legal sanctions; it was reserved for slaves, who were considered to be beneath the level of humanity. The Jews, to whose law it was unknown, had so great a horror of this foreign torture that the odium of it fell upon the whole family of the victim; it became a "house of the crucified." That the victim was stripped of his garments added to the shame. We are loath even to think of this in connection with Jesus. He who is "clothed with light as with a garment,"[344] suffered Himself to be stripped of all save the linen cloth which, after a moment of confusion, was perhaps accorded to Him by a reverent hand. The law seems not to have disallowed this concession; the Jewish usage permitted it — and Mary was there, with the holy women.

[344] Ps. 103:2 (RSV = Ps. 104:2).

But what need is there to add to the humiliation of Jesus by flanking His gibbet, which might well have been a throne of glory, with the crosses of two criminals! Barabbas has been preferred before Him; and now He is ranked with two thieves. Why two? It is possible that the proximity of thieves seemed not enough to shame Him, so that they compensated by doubling the number. Unless perhaps the executioners themselves made this arrangement to save time! In which case, although motive and authors were changed, the insult remains.

As a torture, the cross was a satanic invention; death by a slow fire was less frightful. The victim was nailed to the wood. Think of the effect of square nails, from four to five inches in length, piercing a part of the body so closely packed with nerves and blood vessels as the hands and the feet! The median nerve of the hands was especially affected, and the pain of it throbbed through the whole member.

The feet being nailed flat to the cross, while the knees were bent outwards for the purpose, caused terrible aches and cramp; the position of the whole body made an exhausting demand upon the muscular system. If there was a support for the spine (an *antenna*), the strain would be lessened in this respect, but the local suffering would be increased.

Immobility caused growing contraction of the muscles and increasing congestion. Instinctively the sufferer sought to raise himself upon his hands or feet, trying for some change of position, only to undergo new torments without achieving any relief from his discomfort. Exhaustion soon supervened, but it was an exhaustion without remedy. The victim did not faint; this ruse whereby nature takes refuge from pain in unconsciousness was rendered impossible by the continual twitching of the nerves.

The chest was horribly convulsed; the position of the arms and the tension of the muscles between the ribs caused the victim to gasp for breath; he was slowly suffocated; his heart was overwrought and beat fast but feebly; the blood was thus insufficiently fed, and there was an excess of carbonic acid and an accumulation of waste.

The further effect of this was excitation of the muscular fiber caused by tetanus, and congestion of the brain — that "circle of fire" which made, if one may say so, an inner crown to correspond with the crown of thorns that encircled His head.

The muscles of the neck worked desperately. The head, thrown forward by the crown of thorns, set the body out of the perpendicular, and the sharp points of the thorns pricked and tore the skin. All this increased the cramp, the congestion, and the tetanic convulsions.

Nor must we forget the thirst, that special torture of the wounded. Jesus has drunk nothing since His arrest — nothing, in fact, since the Cenacle. He has been in a constant fever; He has sweated blood; He has been bound; He has been ill treated in the house of Caiaphas; He has carried His Cross in the conditions which we have described; He has refused the drug, and His thirst is still further intensified by the stifling atmosphere.

And now the gasping which causes His mouth to open parches the irritated mucous surfaces even to the lungs. His veins are gradually emptied, if not of blood, at least of any nutritive or refreshing liquid.

The bloodshed, it is surmised, was not very abundant; the wounds of the hands and feet were speedily closed by the clotting of the blood. But the victim gained no advantage from this. The blood retained could find no nourishment, and another kind of hemorrhage supervened, that which the ancient surgeons called the "hemorrhage of pains." A nervous exhaustion comparable to the shedding of blood brought the enfeebled sufferer slowly, and with a cunningly graduated method of torture, to His painful end.

We may understand how the cross can have been called a "bed of terror," and how the contemplation of Jesus suffering this torment has made the mystics cry out with pity. Love is ingenious in constructing its scenes; and the lover reproduces with tormenting fidelity every spasm of his suffering beloved.

It was surely a mystic who inserted in the hymn "Vexilla Regis" ("Soldiers of the King") those supplications to the Cross which show how clearly the essential feature of that torture has been understood: "Bend thy branches, mighty tree, relax the body strained upon thee; be thy natural rigor softened, that the members of the sovereign King may rest more lightly on thy wood!"

These words are the protest of a tender heart; they are the answer to the plaint of the Crucified spoken through the mouth of the prophet: "I am poured out like water; and all my bones are scattered. . . . For many dogs have encompassed me. . . . They have dug my hands and feet. They have numbered all my bones."[345]

But the chief priests of Jerusalem have no pity; they are akin to those who lick the saber with which they have slain an enemy. "Their tongue is a sharp sword," says the Psalm;[346] "their hands are unarmed," adds St. Augustine; "not so their mouth; from thence issues a sword that slays Christ."

This is, in fact, their revenge. He has smitten them pitilessly; He has scourged them with that love "strong as death,"[347] which suffers none to lay hands on the souls that are His. He has refused to be their man, and they have killed Him. They think that thus they save their privileges. And yet the last word has not been spoken. The powers of this world are exhausted, and His death will be their end.

[345] Ps. 21:15, 17-18 (RSV = Ps. 22:14, 16-17).
[346] Ps. 56:5 (RSV = Ps. 57:4).
[347] Song of Sol. 8:6.

∞

Are we to think that their obstinacy excludes them from the benefit of the heavenly words "Father forgive them, for they know not what they do"?[348] No. Jesus excludes none. Even these, in a sense, know not what they do. They do not understand the extent of their crime. Great though it must appear even in their debased conscience, it cannot be appreciated by them for what it is: a universal crime.

Can they see Jesus, living in their midst and opposing them, in the same light as we see Him after nearly twenty centuries of mysterious life, glory, and love? It is more difficult to believe in Jesus when He walks the land of Judea than when He shows Himself as a superhuman King.

The Pharisees see His miracles and do not see His power; God is veiled beneath the man of flesh and blood. They are in bad faith; but for that very reason they need greater faith to believe. They are carnal even as we are, but they have not our helps. Instead, they have their own immediate advantage, prejudices, and reciprocal influences. Who shall say to what extent their conscience is mistaken, and to what extent it is clearly and frankly criminal?

It cannot be denied that Jesus is a revolutionary; His holy revolution is one which must be accepted. But to accept it costs some men so dearly that the reaction of opposed interests and contradicted prejudice may offer some semblance of excuse. Jesus, who knows "what is in man,"[349] who weighs all things in an accurate balance, does not despair of finding even in them something with which He may win His Father's mercy, something upon which He may found His own forgiveness.

[348] Luke 23:34.
[349] John 2:25.

∞

After the mob, turbulent and overtly hostile, cowardly and cruel, behold now the secret sink, the mystery of dark and crafty iniquity, behold Judas. Judas, "one of the Twelve" as the Gospels insistently remind us, Judas the man of Kerioth. "We are told the land of his birth," writes St. John Chrysostom, "whereas we would willingly have not known him at all."

Kerioth is in Judea. Judas is not a Galilean like the others; nevertheless He was called in the same circumstances, incorporated and affiliated to the band at the foot of the mountain, after the prayer.[350]

Although Jesus knew all things, He did not reject him. When a man offers himself, God accepts him. God does not say, "You will not persevere; it is useless for me to receive you." The freedom that makes our decisions binds also a Divine Providence which respects and permits that freedom; freedom is a mystery which seems to tie the hands of God. Under God's government the soul is as independent as though it were alone, but yet as dependent as every other being in regard to its Creator.

Judas holds a definite rank in the apostolic band. He is in charge of the finances; he looks after the money given them for the poor and for their daily needs. The treasurer of this little group is thus treated by the Master with a mark of special confidence. And he is a thief. St. John roundly calls him so.[351]

But a thief who attaches himself to Jesus cannot be any ordinary thief; he is surely something else besides. His vice is begotten of another vice, and his greed must have an object of which money is the symbol rather than the substance.

[350]Luke 6:12-16.
[351]John 12:6.

Jesus distrusts money; He certainly does not allow it to be hoarded, and so there can be little money to steal from Him. But perhaps this founder of the kingdom of Israel may prove to be the purveyor of other desirable things? Money there will be also, no doubt; for greatness brings money. But it will certainly be worthwhile to be one of His disciples when His glory appears.

Judas is an ambitious man. He has not the frankness to say, as the sons of Zebedee said by the mouth of their mother, "I want a high place in the kingdom!"[352] Those two are children; but Judas is a man — a shrewd man. He takes his place unobtrusively in the ranks with the others. He gains their confidence. He will be as devoted to the Master as is necessary; he will not make himself conspicuous. In the meantime the situation will develop and the Master will grow in power. Judas will choose his own way and time for declaring his true object.

He believed in Jesus, did this man! That is, he saw that here was a power which would lead him to great things. He gave himself to Jesus for his own profit. He cast in his lot with the messianic adventure, to which in common with most of his countrymen he attributed a temporal purpose.

The other disciples cherish a similar illusion, and they, too, have their ambitions. But they love; their attachment is generous from the beginning, and if necessary it will be disinterested. Judas does not love at all. This hard heart betrays itself in the house of Simon the Pharisee when, having witnessed a scene such as seldom happens in the history of men, he finds nothing else to say but "wherefore this waste?"[353]

A man who speaks thus passes judgment upon himself. He is below the level of common humanity; he is still more below men

[352] Matt. 20:20-21.
[353] Matt. 26:8; Mark 14:4; John 12:4-5.

of higher aspirations. What, then, is he doing in a group whose whole purpose is a higher life and lofty ideals? He cannot but betray it.

Judas is among the Twelve, but He is not of them. He follows them, but not their sentiments nor those of their Leader. He is there in body, but not in spirit. This "thief" wants to steal the kingdom of God and make it a source of gain. In the meantime he makes his little profits and waits patiently.

But the patience of such men comes to a sudden end. Judas cannot fail to see that the affairs of the little community are taking a bad turn; it becomes more and more evident to him that the path they are following is not his path. He is one of those who must have been very disappointed by the Sermon on the Mount! The constant references to imminent misfortune are so many stabs in his heart, and we can hear him say to himself, "I have been made a fool of! I have been inveigled into a mad enterprise. They promised me a great future, and now I am told that I have sealed my own doom. Away with this man who talks of nothing but death, and away with this ramshackle kingdom of His!"

We have already seen how far disappointment was responsible for the change in the attitude of the Jewish mob; the treason of Judas was attributable to the same cause, in his case much accentuated. Disappointed, Judas becomes bitter; without love, he becomes furious. His enforced self-restraint irks him continually; he broods over his injuries more and more every day. Unable to extricate himself without a shameful confession, perhaps even without danger, he hates.

And here lies the answer to a question which comes to the mind whenever we try to understand this monster of iniquity. If Judas has ceased to be in moral union with Jesus and the Twelve, why does he not withdraw quietly? "This logical course," replied M. Loisy, "is the sort of course that a Judas hardly ever takes. The moral coward who is confronted by a situation which is too difficult for him is usually not content merely to disappear; he tries to avoid it by a base act of violence." This is very true. Judas cannot depart without a crisis. He is too much involved within; he is too much compromised without. What would become of him, labeled in spite of himself as a disciple and having no longer the guarantees of a disciple, the enemy both of the new Israel and of the old, of Jesus and of His accusers?

Salvation, as he understands it, can lie only in one direction, and when we look there we see the terrible temptation that must assail this soul. When two hostile armies confront each other in an enclosed space, what does a soldier do when he intends to desert? He passes over to the enemy. There is no other way out. Having betrayed his friends, he then becomes zealous in the cause of the enemy in order to disarm the mistrust which his treason arouses. He redeems his reputation by going to extremes.

Judas uses exactly the same method. The chief priests are bent upon destroying Jesus. Judas knows this, because Jesus knows it, and in any case it is sufficiently obvious; they are only looking out for an opportunity. Now, these spies beyond the bridge are in reality the secret accomplices of the spy within the camp. Why should he not go and see them? By ranging himself on their side and destroying this ephemeral kingdom by his treason, he will extricate himself from his impossible position and once more be on firm ground.

There are thirty pieces of silver, it is true, and it may be thought that these furnish a sufficient explanation. But upon reflection it seems most unlikely. Thirty pieces of silver are nothing — not more than a few dollars of our money, the price of a slave. It is about the price of the perfume of the Magdalene, and Judas, by his treachery, recoups this "wasted" money. But does this account for an action of such immense consequence?

Setting all question of sentiment aside, there still remains the risk that he must run and the difficulty of finding a way. There may even be sword thrusts; in fact, there will be. Does a man who has waited so long and so patiently expose himself to mortal danger for such a sum as that? No. The money is secondary; it is the streak of meanness in the dark horror of his treachery.

In certain souls even treason may keep its pride; it is careful to observe the proprieties. Here it shows all its habitual baseness and takes a form akin to the commonplace. Judas appears in his treachery as he was in the period of his latent infidelity: avaricious and greedy, coarsely and meanly so, according to his character. One might think that when he agreed upon thirty pieces of silver he was contemplating the first installment of pocket money for the days when he should be free.

∞

When in the supper room Jesus handed the traitor the bread that had been dipped in the dish and thus mysteriously designated him for what he was, St. John remarks, "After the morsel, Satan entered into him."[354] According to St. John Chrysostom, Satan entered a place that was already open. Venerable Bede remarks that he was now entering for the second time, the first time being when Judas decided upon his crime. On the day when he first consented to treachery Satan entered into Judas as into a strange house; now he enters it as his home.

May we not say that he had long been installed there? We may, if we consider what Jesus said a year before, when after the multiplication of the loaves He was explaining the nature of the

[354]John 13:27.

bread of life and the meaning of the divine message. Judas, who on the thirteenth Nisan rose from the table in the midst of the Eucharistic feast, had already shown the blackness of his heart when Jesus promised the living bread.

He was of those who said, "This saying is hard, and who can hear it?"[355] Regarding which St. John makes the comment: "Jesus knew from the beginning who they were that did not believe and who he was, that would betray him."[356] Hence He says, "Have not I chosen you twelve, and one of you is a devil?"[357]

Therefore, for at least a year Jesus has been keeping among His followers a man whom He has unmasked. Yet He treats him exactly as He treats the others. Judas, too, Jesus calls a "friend."[358] Upon him, too, He sheds the light of His soul, allowing him all the rights and privileges of intimacy.

It does not appear that Jesus even refused Judas spiritual assistance, or that He excluded him when, in the days of their enthusiasm, He sent them two by two with the commission to prepare the way for Him,[359] confiding to them the secrets of the kingdom that they might proclaim them, each according to his measure. Yesterday evening He washed his feet; perhaps He might win him by this solemn act of humility. How gently He treats him! We are reminded of the words of the prophet: "The bruised reed He shall not break, and smoking flax He shall not quench."[360]

The attitude of Jesus toward Judas is exactly God's attitude toward every human soul, toward every group of men, toward the

[355] John 6:61.
[356] John 6:65.
[357] John 6:71.
[358] Cf. Matt. 26:50.
[359] Matt. 10:1; Mark 6:7; Luke 9:1-2.
[360] Isa. 42:3.

whole human race: an amazing patience, until the moment when all hope is lost and man has sealed his own doom.

Jesus was patient with Judas, but He was not passive. How often He warned him! The word *devil*, uttered a year before without personal application to him, was an invitation to reflection and repentance. The sorrowful words of yesterday, "You are clean, but not all," were an appeal.[361] "One of you will betray me," was another.[362] And still another was contained in the words "The Son of Man goeth, according as it is written of Him: but woe to that man by whom the Son of Man shall be betrayed."[363]

Jesus is so tactful that even to the last moment the Twelve are wondering "which of them it was that should do this thing."[364] Each of them fears for himself, without any suspicion of the others. But between Jesus and Judas there is no mystery. If He warns His "friend" that his plan is discovered, is it not because Jesus would deter him from it if He could, and bring him to confess and detest the crime while it can still be undone? "What thou dost, do quickly,"[365] He says to him finally; and the traitor, instead of falling at his Master's feet, goes out into the night.

The sign, "Whomsoever I shall kiss, that is He: lay hold on Him quickly,"[366] seems to have been given after he had left the supper room. What sort of soul has this wretch that he can choose as his signal the gesture of love?

Treason is the grief of royalty. Jesus has tasted it now for a long time; He tastes it in all its bitterness on this night. The touch of

---

[361] John 13:10.
[362] John 13:21.
[363] Matt. 26:24.
[364] Luke 22:23.
[365] John 13:27.
[366] Mark 14:44.

the vile mouth of Judas upon His divine face is the last refinement of torture. At other times He has kept silence. But now He makes a remark and opens His soul: "Friend," He says, "whereunto art thou come?"[367] And, looking perhaps straight into his face: "Judas, dost thou betray the Son of Man with a kiss!"[368]

Oh, let the guilty wretch thus entreated consider his act and think who it is that pleads with him! Let that hard heart melt at last in a torrent of tears like Magdalene's! Let the misguided disciple take his proper place once more, be it only under the Cross that he has erected, the Cross upon which Jesus is willing to die for him, giving His blood for him who made it flow! Let him revoke his decision, for there is still time. The prodigal son will be received into the family which is now being instituted, the family which the father, after three days of suffering, will rejoin. He has the right to the fatted calf, the ring, and the white robe. Let him only say the words, "Father, Master, I have sinned against Heaven and against Thee!"[369]

But Judas shuts his heart. He completes his task. And then, seeing the consequences, with that clear vision of realities which comes after the mists of self-deception, he is struck with horror at his crime.

He sees what he has done. For three years he has abused a confidence which was given without reserve. He has repaid that confidence with treachery; he has hastened the end of his friend, his Master. By providing an opportunity for the enemies who were still timid and undecided, he has broken down the dike that stemmed the torrent of hatred, iniquity, and cruelty. When he left the Cenacle his departure was the beginning of death for Jesus.

[367]Matt. 26:50.
[368]Luke 22:48.
[369]Luke 15:18.

Having introduced a disturbing note into the final familiar discourse of the Master, he went out to deliver Him to death. Having tasted love in its most delicate and generous manifestation, he chose the symbol of love as the sign of his treason.

The ancient writers compare him to Joab who with one hand held the chin of Amasa to kiss him, while with the other he plunged a dagger into his side.[370] Judas does not set his own hand to the sword. He is afraid of direct action; he bids the soldiers bind his Master and "lead him away carefully."[371]

True, Judas thus conferred a great benefit upon the universe; by hastening the Passion he set in motion the work of our salvation. His betrayal incites us to reparation and gives a treasure to our love. "It was a good bargain for us," writes one of the early Church fathers. "Judas sells Him, the Jews buy Him, and we receive the Savior." "Since Jesus is for sale," writes another, "let us buy Him with our hearts."

But the consequences change nothing in the sentiments or in the responsibility of the traitor. The deed of Judas remains what it is; Jesus represents it to Pilate as the most heinous crime of all, because it is the most decisive and the most sacrilegious. And now Judas himself sees it in all its stark and hideous reality.

∞

Once Jesus has been condemned to death the man of Kerioth seems to recoil from his cruel work. Without repenting in the moral sense of the word, he appears to renounce the fruits of his

---

[370] 2 Kings 20:9-10 (RSV = 2 Sam. 20:9-10). Among the Jews it was the custom sometimes, as it still is among the Arabs and the Persians today, to hold a man's beard when kissing him.

[371] Mark 14:44.

crime. His money scorches him; his ambition is stifled by remorse; the implicit accusation that he has made against his Master by delivering him up becomes an intolerable thought. He goes to the Jews. "I have sinned," he says, "betraying innocent blood," and brings back the thirty pieces of silver, as though expecting that they must in return release their victim. The priests scoff at him. "What is that to us? See thou to it!"[372]

Then, seeing himself repulsed, left to his own resources and not finding in his heart the stuff of which true repentance is made, Judas becomes a prey to dark despair. The feeling of his moral desolation appalls him. He is seized with a desire to fly, and the infinity of space seems not enough for his flight. He shuns the Temple, he shuns the city, he shuns life itself, for which he has no further desire. Impulsively he casts the thirty pieces of silver to the ground, and the field of Akeldama, "the field of blood," will immortalize his crime.[373]

Unhappy wretch! What did he hope to gain for the healing of his soul by going to the priests? Why in his distress did he have recourse to this Hell where no charity was on the watch for his coming? Did he hope to find redemption among scoundrels? Are hatred and brutality balm for a wounded heart?

Judas repents, the Gospel tells us. He repents, but instead of coming to Him who alone can accept his repentance and render it efficacious, he remains with his own self and turns to his accomplices. He wants to be rid of these monsters without attaching himself to Jesus. He is disgusted with himself, but will not confide in his Master. He wants to find cleansing water apart from the fountain of life, and finding himself cast out, he sees his only refuge in death.

[372] Matt. 27:4.
[373] Matt. 27:6-8; Acts 1:18-19.

That is his final crime.

In the eyes of Jesus all things can be pardoned. Do we not see it in the case of the poor repentant thief who, when he has understood that Life is his neighbor, turns to It with such moving simplicity?

"Dost thou not fear God?" he says to the thief who is blaspheming, "seeing thou art under the same condemnation. And we indeed justly, for we receive the due reward of our sins; but this man hath done no evil." Turning to the Master, he adds, "Lord, remember me when Thou shalt come into Thy kingdom!"[374] He speaks to Him familiarly; he is addressing a companion in misfortune. Is Jesus not nailed to the Cross, like himself? "My brother in suffering," he seems to say, "will You not have regard to my repentance and make me Your brother in glory?" The divine heart cannot resist such a transport of confidence. The poor Jew, speaking of the kingdom's glory, seems only to have in mind the second coming of the Messiah. But Heaven's pardon is munificent: "This day," Jesus answers, "thou shalt be with me in Paradise."[375]

This is the Savior's way. He seems to have been awaiting that final appeal. At the very first word His answer is ready. He does not deliberate; He adds a codicil to His will and bequeaths to this poor wretch the riches of His kingdom.

And this is the lesson of Judas: in the eyes of Jesus all things can be pardoned, all, save the refusal of pardon itself. This refusal is a supreme blasphemy. It denies the supreme goodness. It means a mistrust which is the cruelest insult that love can suffer, an insult which itself implies the total absence of love.

And so it all comes back to this: Judas does not love. He does not love and that is why he betrays. He does not love, and that is

[374]Luke 23:40-42.
[375]Luke 23:43.

why, having cast aside treason because it horrifies him, he ends by detesting himself without repenting. Self-hatred is salutary only when associated with the love of God. Alone it is homicidal; it has the power to destroy everything and it has no power at all to repair.

In that moment, having failed to understand the heart of his Master and finding no help of any kind in his own, Judas came to the conclusion that there was no longer room for him among men. He hanged himself this morning, haggard and alone — more than alone, for he had emptied himself of himself. He hanged himself on Good Friday! He is raised up between Heaven and earth, like Jesus, and yet in how different a way! He is foreign to Heaven and to earth, and he separates them. Jesus belongs to the one and to the other, and He joins them together.

∞

From the Cross, since here all is forgiveness and redemptive suffering, Jesus does not curse the disciple who has gone astray. He has no anger in His heart; but He leaves him "in his own place," according to those terrible words of the Acts,[376] for he had made his choice between that place and Calvary. The Eleven are on Calvary, either in person or in their representative; they are there in heart. Judas is not there. Jesus does not see him; Jesus, sadly, forsakes him. With sorrowful majesty He withdraws His gaze from one who has fled Him with an everlasting flight. He has no glance for the "son of perdition."[377]

[376] Acts 1:25.
[377] 2 Thess. 2:3.

9

His Tomb

When Jesus crossed the threshold of the Gate of Ephraim, He was in the condition of the martyr who is thrust into the arena. The martyr looks into the lion's jaws; Jesus saw His tomb, and its yawning mouth must have reminded Him of the text of Job: "My spirit is wasted, my days are shortened, and only the grave remaineth for me."[378]

Nevertheless, as our Lord looked beyond, another perspective opened before Him; He could say confidently with David His ancestor, "Thou wilt not leave my soul in Hell; nor wilt Thou give Thy Holy One to see corruption. Thou hast made known to me the ways of life."[379]

There is a symbolic beauty in the circumstance that the tomb of Jesus was only a few paces from His Cross. Suffering and death are but two aspects of the same thing; the one lays us low, and the

---

[378] Job 17:1.
[379] Ps. 15:10-11 (RSV = Ps. 16:10-11).

other completes the work of destruction. Yet through Jesus they both raise us up, and our joint ascension presents the three stages of the Cross, the tomb, and Heaven.

∞

Jewish tombs were commonly placed in gardens, and this garden district on the outskirts of the city contained many of them. Some of them remain to this day and it is quite easy to imagine how they were disposed.

The chambers of the sepulcher were hewn out of the bare rock. The ancient Israelites built little, but they excavated much; they gained thus both in space and in the durability of their work. It is for this reason that their burial places have lasted longer than their cities. Many ancient sites can now be traced only by means of holes in the rocks, with steps leading to the mouths of the caves.

In the time of Jesus there was special activity with pick and chisel. In addition, we find decorative work inspired by Graeco-Roman technique. Characteristic specimens are to be found in the valley of Jehoshaphat and in the region of Abud, Timnah, and elsewhere. The visitor who studies these with the Gospels in hand may find the elements of a vivid "composition of place" for his meditations.

The exterior aspect of the tombs varies from the simple hole, square or rectangular, to the isolated pyramidal structure, surrounded by a trench and sometimes surmounted by a dome. Between these two extremes the whole gamut of moldings, scrolls, rosettas, crosses, garlands, imitation pillars, and columns serves to indicate the luxury or the pride, the piety or the taste of the owners of the tomb.

In nearly every case the monument comprises a vestibule, which is either a roofed space preceded by columns or an open courtyard. This last contrivance became necessary when the excavation was made upon a slight slope, as in the case of Calvary. The forecourt is then a leveled area, suitable for solitary meditation or for family reunions. In the wall beyond, a low door is cut, leading into the burial chamber, or else into an anteroom connecting with one or more chambers, provided with *arcosolia*,[380] shafts,[381] stone benches, or shelf graves.

By comparing the details given in the Gospel accounts with the topographical and archaeological data, it is possible to form a very accurate idea of what Joseph of Arimathea's tomb was like, what our Holy Sepulcher originally was.

Access was gained to it by a trench, which would be fairly long by reason of the gradual slope. Its length was lessened, and its depth increased, by means of steps leading down from the threshold to a vestibule on a lower level. In front was a low door leading into a first chamber destined for burial rites: the washing of the body, embalming, and prayers. Beyond, another low door opened into the tomb proper, the wall being pierced to the right by a vaulted niche to receive the body.

It is not known whether provision had been made for other bodies. It was always possible to hew out other graves whenever they were needed. This was the advantage of the system: it was possible without disturbing the bodies already buried there to enlarge the sepulcher indefinitely by digging farther on into the mountainside.

The lower stratum of the sacred niche would be hollowed into a slight curve; a stone pillow was placed to support the head. Of such thoughtful provision we find occasional traces today: the

[380] Vaulted trough-tombs.

[381] Tombs hewn in the rock in such a way that the body is thrust in shaftwise.

motivating idea for these arrangements was that the dead must be comfortable to be able to sleep. The two chambers were on a lower level than the passages of approach, so that the burial cave might be deeper. The first room would contain a circular stone bench and an open space in the middle for convenience in passing to and fro and for purposes of embalming.

Regarding the manner of opening and closing the tomb there can be little doubt. When they reach the tomb the holy women say to one another, "Who shall roll away the stone?"[382] The stone in question is a millstone such as may still be seen in the Tomb of the Kings or the Tomb of the Herods, at Abu Ghosh, at Nablus, and elsewhere. These millstones may sometimes weigh more than a ton. That of the Tomb of the Herods weighs even more, and we are told that the stone of our Savior's tomb was "very great."[383]

The process can be easily imagined. On the outer side of the open door is a groove to receive the millstone as it is moved in front of the opening or away from it. When the tomb is closed the stone fits against the right wall, which is slightly grooved to receive it; it is kept in position by wedges. To open it, the wedges are removed and the stone, which has been levered up a slight slope into its groove in the wall, rolls down again by its own momentum into a groove to the left. Clearly such a maneuver was beyond the strength of the holy women; at least two men were required. To remove the wedges the stone had to be pushed up a little; then it had to be eased down the slope. Not only would women have run the risk of hurting themselves, but they had no authority to act alone.

All the preparations mentioned in the Gospel account had been made simultaneously with the grave. Therefore everything

[382] Mark 16:3.
[383] Mark 16:4.

was at hand on Good Friday, so that there is no need to think that Joseph of Arimathea had foreseen what was going to happen. It appears, in fact, that he had not; St. John tells us that they were forced to act as they did by the imminence of the Sabbath, and by the proximity of this tomb.[384]

What an honor for Joseph of Arimathea! He becomes akin to the Cyrenean: Simon carries the Cross, Joseph carries the Crucified. And Nicodemus, the doctor of the nocturnal interview,[385] buys a hundred pounds of aloes and myrrh to garnish the somber cave in which he will have his last meeting with Jesus.[386] But the hasty embalming of Friday is merely the provisional work of those pious hands; on the day after the Sabbath a solemn embalming will take place. But when that time comes an angel will appear to say what has to be said, and will tell the women of the miracle.

∽

How clearly all this must appear before the mind of the divine Master, and what feelings it must arouse in His heart! From the Cross He can no longer see the tomb, but He feels it drawing Him. He is conscious of its nearness; He thinks of its importance for His work. He needs it in order to take the rest of the busy worker who looks forward to the task that awaits him at dawn. There He is to lay down His life and there He is soon to take it up again; for a moment He lays down His burden of love.

When He says "It is consummated,"[387] Jesus is thinking of the tomb. His words are a commentary upon the effects of the Cross

[384]John 19:42.
[385]John 3:1-2.
[386]John 19:39.
[387]John 19:30.

as well as upon the Cross itself and what has prepared the way for it. This rock cave is to furnish His most convincing manifestation, His "sign." It is His proof, and it is His final gift.

The burial is the completion of the Passion. For the enemies of Jesus it is their last pursuit of Him; for Him it is the final abasement, the ultimate sacrifice. When we go to the tomb we give what we cannot keep; it is our final fall. Jesus gives a life of which He is still the master, and He makes His own the power of God.

He intends by His tomb to set a seal upon His work, and the Synagogue helps in spite of itself by setting a seal on His tomb. This tomb is the last picture in the illustrated Gospel, the final symbol connected with the sublime reality of redemption. With such a picture to drive it home, the word of the Son of Man will never be forgotten, the eternal significance of His message will never be disputed. His disciples will no more be able to sleep, nor will generations, nor history. A new principle of regeneration has been inserted in the human race and life will blossom once more. Henceforth there will be only one great event in the course of ages: that which ends and begins in the sacred cave.

Nor does this concern man alone. The Passion is intended for our salvation; but it is also an act of worship. When Jesus comes down from the Cross into the arms of His loved ones and from thence passes to the tomb, He will reach the extremity of adoration. He must go thus far for His Father's honor. Descending to the depths He will give the highest glory love can give. In abandoning Himself to the uttermost limits of nothingness He will praise His Father by giving Him occasion for the noblest of His works.

On Easter morning there will appear the power of Him "that quickeneth the dead and calleth those things that are not."[388] The

---

[388]Rom. 4:17.

wisdom of His plans will then be seen. The love that inspires that wisdom will be met by an equal love, which will recognize it for what it is: a love manifested to the uttermost, a divine love which is a model for all. It is the love that gives.

∞

The idea of sacrifice must not allow us to set aside all thought of the glories to come; it is these which in the mind of Jesus give its real meaning to the tomb.

Jesus is the Lord of time. From the Cross He sees every phase of it. He experiences that thrill of the future which stirs the prophets. Reading in the book of eternity He sees the events of the morrow that is coming.

He dies; His body is laid in the tomb; the myrrh and aloes diffuse their scent abroad; the band of holy women keep silent guard; the angels watch; the sentinels of the Sanhedrin think with their seals to master the power of Heaven; on the third morning the rock splits and cracks; the sun of Easter morning rises; mysterious words pass between the messenger and the holy women; the deserted region rings with the footsteps of Peter and John as they run; tidings of joy warm the hearts of the disciples and dry their tears; the mystery of life after death is inaugurated; the two men of Emmaus walk in the dusk of evening; the last fishing boat rocks at anchor; the angels of the Ascension look down from above, stoles crossed on their breasts.

Sorrows are busily preparing for joy, and the seven words of anguish do not drown the words by which the Church is founded, words that will soon be solemnly repeated. The arms extended on the Cross prefigure the gesture with which Jesus will send the Twelve to the four corners of the earth.

∞

Surrexit Christus, spes mea! "Christ, my hope, is risen!" This tomb which is the hope of the world is also, and especially on Calvary, the hope of Christ. Let us, then, think first of Him, who can no more forget His humanity than we can forget our own. He is suffering; He has no wish not to suffer. He submits willingly to death; but this does not mean that He does not look forward to the end of His suffering after His work is done.

"In the evening weeping shall have place, in the morning gladness."[389] The evening traverses the night and goes forth to meet the day. . . .

∞

For us the grave is a dungeon in which we are forgotten until the end of time. Our soul escapes it, but our body falls to dust, and we are lost to remembrance. The tomb of Christ is merely a passing phase, like an underground passage ending in a triumphal arch. Jesus uses it as the gate of death; but straightaway He makes it a gate of life.

While the grave claims us for the whole duration of the world, Christ pays but a grudging tribute to its demands. Two days, and this tombstone will be broken like an eggshell. Two days, and this cave will open like a pair of lips, and life will come forth like a divine smile.

Pascal has remarked that "Jesus Christ worked no miracles in the grave."[390] The miracle comes afterward. The miracle consists first in the Resurrection, and then in this marvelous life after

---

[389] Ps. 29:6 (RSV = Ps. 30:5).
[390] Pascal, *Pensées*, no. 735 in *Oeuvres complètes*, 1311.

death, of which the Spirit that He has left us is the animating principle, of which the whole universe is the theater.

∞

> The soldiers of the king march forth
> The mystery of the Cross shines on.[391]

Is not this the "government" which "is upon His shoulder"?[392] Is not this the empire which shall rest upon the shoulder that bent beneath the Cross? The Cross has taken flight like an eagle. It will dart from one end of our horizon to the other, and wherever it shines the soul will find its home and Jesus His kingdom.

If it is true that "history is the science of events which have a posterity," then Jesus must be said to dominate the whole of history. Marvels begin to succeed each other as soon as He is risen. After the Passion of the Gospel comes the action of the Acts. After the Resurrection comes the enthusiasm of the great witnesses and Apostles, the faith of the wonder-workers mingled with that of their beneficiaries: the shadow of Peter that heals the sick; the heavens that open above the head of Stephen; the beneficent thunderbolt on the road to Damascus; the conquest that begins slowly, spreads, and is consolidated; the churches that are formed and make communion with each other; the unity that is enriched by its concentration and strengthened by its richness; the civil society that reacts, persecutes, and then yields; the world that is won over little by little, until by the fourth century all that has a name in the civilized world finds itself to be Christian.

In the sequel there will be vicissitudes, for no force constrains our freedom. We have said that in contrast to the desires of the

[391] Vexilla regis prodeunt / Fulget crucis mysterium.
[392] Isa. 9:6.

205

Son of Man the results of His work may be called a reverse. However, if we assess *what is* instead of lamenting *what is not*, then we must see in this same future an immense regeneration.

It must not be forgotten that in the eyes of the impartial observer Christianity and true civilization are synonymous. Light recedes as Christ recedes: it advances in step with Him. History has two facets. In the garden of Gethsemane Jesus saw the facet of darkness; on the Cross, looking beyond the tomb, He saw the facet of light.

∞

Finally, there are events closer at hand which attract the gaze of the Crucified as the form of the tomb appears before Him. Jesus sees in advance all that will come to pass after the Sabbath that is now approaching: the persistent malevolence of His persecutors; their intervention with Pilate to ensure careful watch upon the tomb; the deceit and the bribery of the guards when the miracle has become known. But one prefers to suppose that His thoughts are content to remain with His loved ones, and that without overlooking their early distress, their broken hopes, and their hesitations, He especially foresees their joy.

His loved ones will think that they have lost Him, as Mary and Joseph had lost Him in the Temple. Then, just as in the Temple He had been found in conversation with the doctors, so He will set an end, by a miraculous meeting with them, to His conversation with death.

On Calvary there were few friends, and these were especially women. At the tomb there will be few witnesses, and they will be especially women. Before their departure this evening they will note the arrangements of the tomb in view of their return. They will mount silent guard. They will purchase spices for the final embalming, and they will come at the first hour after the Sabbath to perform their loving task on behalf of us all.

They will find the vestibule open. They will remark the presence of heavenly beings. But the great Absent One of whom alone they are thinking will seem to be lost to them once more, and they will run breathlessly to bear the news to the Twelve. The mystery of what has occurred will not be far from their minds. It will be in their hopes and thoughts; yet their anguish will not be dispelled until, after repeated appearances of the Master, the light of Easter shines clearly upon them.

ॐ

It is at this point that we must place the episode of Mary Magdalene, an episode linked with that of the tomb of Lazarus, with that of Simon's house, and with that of Calvary.

She was there, Magdalene with the two other Marys, women one with her in name and heart. Despite the angelic light, despite an announcement which for a less troubled spirit would have been perfectly clear, she saw nothing save only this: they have taken her Lord and she does not know "where they have laid Him."[393]

Faced with a crime which has robbed her of her last treasure, that dear yet heartrending object of her tender love, she is like a body without soul. She sees, and yet she does not see; she hears and yet she does not hear; she is not where she is, but where He is. Such is her distraught state of mind when she asks the supposed gardener, "Tell me where thou hast laid Him?"[394]

She speaks with a sort of piteous, haggard violence. She breaks into impetuous words. She has no fear; one fears only when one

[393] John 20:13.
[394] John 20:15.

loves, and now that her Love is gone, there is nothing in the world for Magdalene to love.

Jesus reveals Himself by speaking only one word, in the tone she alone could tell: "Mary!" She recognizes Him by the sweetness of that name. "Mary!" He names Himself in naming her; within "Mary" she hears "Jesus," so often has she heard that name coming from the lips and from the heart of her divine Beloved. Magdalene can only answer with an echo: "*Rabboni!* Master!"[395]

She would have rushed to Him; He restrains her with a gesture. A sublime reserve is called for at this unique moment, midway between life and survival, between earth and Heaven. But love has made itself known and eternal words have been exchanged. He who names beings for all eternity has called her His beloved, and she has acclaimed Him as her Master.

And thus ends Magdalene's lesson for us. She teaches us the omnipotence of tears and the omnipotence of love. By her tears she earned her own forgiveness, the resurrection of a dear brother, an anticipated union with the Passion, and the joy of the glorious tomb. She was the first to understand, and so she was the first to receive the mission of announcing the good news. She is the Apostle of the Apostles. This is love's privilege. And so it will be in the course of Christian history. Love will play a part which in some ways is more important than that of any authority, power, or learning.

∞

What happens for Magdalene happens proportionately for all those who share her sentiments and her task. The other holy

---

[395] John 20:16.

women are so closely associated with their sister that it is difficult to see, from the Gospels, what is proper to Magdalene alone and what is common to the whole group. The disciples have their part, and, as one would expect, it is a predominant part in decisive events. All have a happy part to play. Hearts rise from the dead, and yet in all we find a strange astonishment and the imperfections of a vacillating faith.

Is there one perfect among them? Yes, one. Mary, the sublime Mother, tastes in secret the fullness of joy regained, having given proof of model virtue in her time of trial. She rises from her Compassion, as Jesus rises from His Passion, as Magdalene rises from her desolation, as the Apostles rise from their fear and utter weariness.

If the Gospel is silent concerning her, it is not because it has forgotten her, but because it cannot tell. An exquisite sentiment would have us veil a mystery so tender, lest words taint its charm. The silence that hovers over Mary, far from meaning that she is neglected, serves only to emphasize her greatness.

10

Heaven

In the eyes of the dying Savior, things and people are never withdrawn from their natural environment nor isolated from the divine sphere in which they are enclosed. When He meditates upon what He sees He cannot but consider its divine content. Heaven envelops the earth and all things that are upon it. Lifted up from the earth, more by His soul than by His Cross, Christ finds in Heaven the first object of His contemplation. From Heaven He comes and to Heaven He returns. Thus it is with His eyes raised to Heaven that we must think of Him uttering His first and His last sentences, each of them beginning with the word *Father*.

In saying this we are not confusing the material heavens with that of which they are the symbol. We intend merely to stress the striking character of that symbol, the inevitable association in our minds between those azure heights of the sky and the sublime things of the spirit.

The blue vault of the heavens represents for us the extreme of height. The whole order in which we are involved seems caught up in its whirling cycle; our destinies are governed by it. The eternal works and their Workman shine there incessantly; the future life to which we aspire seems to dawn in its depths.

And so it is natural that Heaven should have its part in all our sentiments, especially in their extremes; and with Jesus it is the same as with us all. When we are in quest of sublime and holy awe, Heaven offers us its nights. In our distress it is toward Heaven that we raise our arms. When we affirm we take Heaven as our witness. Our loves and our hates invoke it. Our conception of the necessary is symbolized by its indefectibility. And when others would console us it is in Heaven's name that they speak.

God Himself, who always condescends to our ways of conceiving things, connects the spiritual lessons which He wishes to convey and the spiritual events which He governs, with the phenomena of the heavens. It is to Heaven that His elect ascend: from Elijah in the fiery chariot[396] to Christ Himself and the Blessed Mother. From Heaven the Son of Man will come heralded by trumpets of archangels. Yahweh speaks with thunder as with His own voice. His realm is the ether; His tabernacle is the sun; the clouds and the winds are His messengers; the slow sunrise is His glance; and in the silence of the stars He would have the believer hear a hymn of praise to their Maker.

Sometimes the heavens are called in Scripture the "upper room" of God,[397] and the sacred writer — and Jesus also — is anxious that the sublime domain should not lose this meaning in our imaginations.

What becomes of man if he forgets that there above a Father is on the watch; that the lights of Heaven reveal His presence; that its laws are the expression of His Providence; that the great nameless temple has Him for its guest, the same guest who dwells

[396] 4 Kings 2:11 (RSV = 2 Kings 2:11).
[397] Ps. 103:2-3, 13 (RSV = Ps. 104:2-3, 13).

in the temple of our hearts? The failure to recognize this is man's prime infidelity. It is because they turn away from God that men cease to understand nature's message and often credit it with a language which is blasphemy. As soon as we turn to the first Love, all that was once a veil becomes revealing.

Likewise the expression Jesus Himself created, "heavenly Father,"[398] reminds us of the fatherhood of God, and emphasizes the loving character and the religious meaning of the created universe, this sublime outer garment of the divinity which St. Peter in his account of the Transfiguration calls the "excellent glory."[399]

Only so can we know the tragic aspect of the world, can its events reveal. Its dread immensity no longer terrifies; its silence does not bewilder. The wide view that boundless space imposes, contrasting so violently with our puny activity, gives birth only to a great religious peace. All is reassurance and all is instruction.

I am lost in the universe, but in God I find myself again, and I cannot stray out of this ample bosom, outside of which is nothing. Invisible arms support the horizon; I feel the life of my infinite God. I understand that the "inaccessible" is close to us, that "the inexorable" has a soul and that to that soul our own is akin: "We are also His offspring."[400] And so I am fearless when at evening I open my window on the gulf of darkness. But how inhuman and how false the night would be if it did not speak to us of God!

∞

It is not without importance at the foot of the Cross, which reconciles all extremes, to notice how the heavens — especially

---

[398] Matt. 6:26; Luke 11:13.

[399] 2 Pet. 1:17.

[400] Acts 17:28.

the heavens at night — are related to the mystery of the soul. The ether is beyond all measure; and beyond all measure and understanding also are the stirrings of the heart. We cannot rise to the stars nor descend to the depths of our being. Two infinites stretch beyond the bounds of our experience, and both attract us irresistibly yet hold us at a distance.

What can we do without God in the heights, and without His grace in the depths of ourselves? Yet we feel that these two domains coalesce and that God, who is in us and ineffably beyond us, welds the whole of nature into one. If we go to God and give ourselves to Him, then we can reconcile all things — being, our own being, and the Subsistent Being upon whom all else depends.

We cannot doubt that Christ always has an intimate realization of these things. If "the Father had given all things into His hands,"[401] it was assuredly with the full consciousness that this was so. Filled with the knowledge of what is, He has by that very fact full assurance in what He does. His vision reaches unerringly to God, the living Heaven, to the soul, that lowly heaven in which the other is reflected, to the nature of the universe, and to Himself in whom all these fragments of reality find their unity.

What can we say here that will not be in vain? Is not all explanation foredoomed to futility? Who shall put into words the state of the soul of Christ as He raises His eyes to Heaven? Yet it is good to attempt even the impossible: description may fail, but contact will bear fruit. Let us say the things of which we are certain, keeping before our minds always those wide vistas which

[401] John 3:35.

open out when we pronounce that word which is so simple and yet so charged with harmonious significance: *Heaven*.

∞

Jesus loved the beauties of nature. The blue vault of the heavens, its bright array of clouds, its mysterious night, its changing reflections which our things of earth pick up and flash to and fro: He who was in all things the Son of Man could not be indifferent to these wonders.

One delights to think of Jesus in the midst of the beauty of the world, contemplating it as a mystic and expressing it as a poet, in a mute thought of which we are given a glimpse in the restrained eloquence of His parables. The vision of His mind is not limited to this sublunar world, nor even to the firmament with its countless suns. But the immediate environment to which His mortal flesh is akin, which is the measure as well as the object of His senses, which gives food to His imagination, and which takes hold of His memory, is nonetheless in the foreground of His human thought.

He casts a loving glance upon this portion of the heavens which we call earth. He is its son. Turning toward its Source, He gives it in love all that He can receive from it, as He has received from it all that it can give. Nature enchants Him and raises Him to ecstasy: "See the lilies of the field, how they grow! . . . Amen I say to you, that not Solomon in all his glory was arrayed like one of these."[402]

Fervently, in common with His disciples, He recites the prayer in the Temple: "I behold Thy heavens, the works of Thy fingers:

[402] Matt. 6:28-29.

the moon and the stars which Thou hast founded."[403] His discourses are full of the fields, the threshing ground, the mill, the
beehive, the house, the open sheepfold with its watchtower, the
fig tree and the olive tree, the vine branch and the grape that is
pressed under foot. In them we can hear the swallows and the
pigeons; the dog begging its bread like a humble supplicant; the
hen dreading the eagle and the storm for her little ones as He
Himself fears for humanity. His message is wrapped in earthly
symbols, and instinctively He chooses the most beautiful, which
are also the most familiar, those whose simple grandeur is the basis
of human poetry.

And yet He is not the aesthete pure and simple; He is all truth
and all action. But truth has her handmaids, and without devoting
Himself entirely to these, Jesus uses them to the extent that they
serve His spiritual purpose.

Never does the general impression of the world leave Him; and
when He quits the world He will have set upon it the imprint of
His thought. Nature will be richer in meaning, more spiritually
eloquent, more charged with life, as it will also be a more fervent
adorer, animated by the Christian spirit.

Who better than this human and heavenly soul was able to
taste God in the universe and the universe in the God who
sustains it? Associated with the divine harmony (One in Three,
Three in One), is He not wholly attuned to the music of creation?
Son of Man, does He not find in man's dwelling place His proper
home? He has caught up in Himself the whole of humanity. He
bears within Himself the Idea, the begetter of beings. He is the
"beginning of the creation of God"[404] and He is the End. Everything is a symbol of Him. Nature tends to Him with all its

---

[403] Ps. 8:4 (RSV = Ps. 8:3).
[404] Rev. 3:14.

significance and all its powers. Can He help loving this patrimony, this mirror, this outcome of the Idea which is Himself, this world, God's altar of repose?

The beauty which merely drugs the pagan soul with languid rapture, rivets the thoughts of Jesus upon His Father. And His adoration of the Father, which causes the narrow mystic to forget the universe, turns His mind to created beauty once again.

He perceives the harmony of creation as an eternal Will whose applications to human life form the object of His teaching, of His exhortations, and of His grace. He mingles Heaven with earth, nature with the soul, time with the eternal outcome of time. For these extremes are connected, and of each of these kingdoms He is citizen.

∞

We said that in contemplating nature the thought of Jesus is not limited to the little that is visible to us. His vision of the heavens is not bounded by our horizons. Heaven is the blue firmament; but heaven is also the assembly of all the worlds. Beyond these great witnesses and between them is the ether in which they swim, that unknown element which they traverse and by which they are traversed, an amazing stream which even our thought can hardly conceive and which is quite unknown to the senses. How far this sea extends with its harmonious waves, where this perpetual marvel comes to an end, no man knows. But Christ, united with His Father as Word and as Mediator, with Him "telleth the number of the stars" and the spheres, "and calleth them all by their names."[405]

---

[405] Ps. 146:4 (RSV = Ps. 147:4).

In the opposite direction, down in the depths of being, in the heart of substances and events, the infinitely tiny — and these are also worlds — open heavens no less vast to the vision of Christ. Atoms are stars, and it may be that our stars are the atoms of bodies vaster still, as Pascal believed.

This vastness piled upon vastness, the thought of which fills us with terror and seems to make us nothing, has Christ for its witness and its judge. In His mind is written the law of these worlds, which is the law of all things. The wisest of us are blind in these immensities, but His thought suffers none of the narrowness or infirmity of ours. In the contemplation of Christ all boundaries are effaced. He penetrates Being from end to end. He ascends from heaven to heaven and He descends from abyss to abyss. His vision carries as far as His Father's power. His ecstasy is akin to the breath of the Creator that causes the fertile earth to stir with life and wakens all lands to spring.

∞

Are we to suppose that these visions are clouded on the Cross, and that Heaven no longer shines for the sorrowing Savior? To think so would be a delusion and almost an offense. More than once we have spoken of that clairvoyance of the dying, of that flood of memories that seems as though it would strive to fill the void which death will create. In Jesus more than in anyone else, on Golgotha as in Gethsemane, all the pictures of life pass and pass again, natural impressions are reborn, and far from vanishing, are more vivid than before.

At the moment of the great death Heaven and earth will make a demonstration; their tumult will protest against the crime of men. Is it not just that He who dies should also salute nature, His faithful servant?

He accepted the perfumes of Magdalene as heralding His burial. Surely the scents that rise from the earth on this day of spring, those of the lilies that form a carpet on the rocks, those borne on the breezes from Jericho and wafted to the Cross, will have the same significance and receive from Him a similar welcome?

To all the glory of this land of grey rocks, to that of every land where people dwell, and to all the beauties of the universe which are His, the Word Incarnate does honor as He dies, just as in life He received their obeisance. The blue sky, the green hills, and the flowers offer Him the colors of His Father. The picture of the world which He drew Himself, a picture so beautiful and so true, is before Him even as He dies on the Cross.

∽

Admittedly the Cross is dark amidst these visions. But it is the Cross that brought them, because it is for the Cross that He came "who was to come,"[406] and it is on His way to this tragic night that He has passed through this splendid aurora.

And so Jesus can still contemplate the beauties of nature as He dies. He does not cast them aside; there is no gloom in His sorrow. His sorrow is glorious and calm, and the splendor within rejoices in the beauty that envelops Him without. He dies in springtime. The flight of birds encompasses Him about; the voice of the turtledoves echoes His sighs. From His soul He hails His Galilee, His Judea, the green fields of Samaria that unite them, and the earth, the casket in which these jewels are set. He gazes into a space that stretches far beyond the little corner of earth that He has trod, and He is dazzled by the distant vision. The dark cloud

[406] Matt. 3:11; Luke 3:16.

that is soon to extend will be but a gossamer veil. The anemones of Golgotha, seen in a false light, had brightened their vermilion tint as He ascended the hill. Now they range their thick clusters like a constellation around the foot of the Cross, and there, in the distance, on the earthen roofs of the houses, are numberless other anemones, while numberless poppies and marguerites — white and red stars with hearts of gold — spread a flowery heaven before His gaze.

For everything that Jesus sees is Heaven to Him; to Jesus all things are Heaven. Nature is heavenly in its surface and in its depths, in its heights and in its abysses, in its gorgeous array and in its substance. The divine attributes there reflected find similar attributes in Jesus, and no one can contemplate them better than He is able to.

About the Cross, Heaven is everywhere, for Jesus sees all things as drowned, yet undimmed, in the sea of immensity; as implicated, yet not lost, in the eternal design.

∞

One aspect of this heavenly vision needs to be considered apart. It is only in appearance that it is distinct from the rest, or at the most by external signs. Yet in our eyes it is outstanding and calls for a special study — a bold study indeed if we intended to make definitions. But we intend only to adore, and with a few reverent words to set a barrier around a zone of silence.

Jesus prays. His prayer on the Cross is a continuation of His constant prayer. If the sky is Heaven, if the universe, the soul, and God are Heaven, then the act by which Jesus links all of these together in one common thought is a communion with Heaven in the most complete sense of the word, a vision of Heaven boundless and sublime.

The habitual prayer of Jesus is an anticipated fulfillment of the precept of His Apostle: "Pray without ceasing."[407] And this means that in Him desire is always directed toward God, that the Spirit with His "unspeakable groanings"[408] never ceases to inflame and to offer to the Father every aspiration of His will.

∞

Jesus' ordinary speech prays; His silence prays; His very being prays. Under the two forms which are prescribed for us, prayer is the whole basis of the divine Master's life. All His acts, even the most obscure, are nothing but a long solemn and perfect adoration. As a victim offered for all time, He is a living prayer.

However, since He leads this life of ours and wills to serve as its model He cannot omit those visible and periodical acts which sanctify that life and enhance it. He prays at set times; He prays in the Temple and in the synagogue; in addition He prays three times a day, after the manner of the Jews. He prays longer in the evening, in the open air, often upon the hills, and this last prayer expressly associates with the transports of His heart that heavenward glance which we see upon the Cross.

∞

The Gospel has painted this wondrous picture for us: Jesus alone on a mountain, His eyes turned toward the immensity of space, at one moment perhaps prostrate, at another with His arms crossed, praying with His whole being, and especially with His whole soul, while the heavens pray with all their stars.

[407] 1 Thess. 5:17.
[408] Rom. 8:26.

When evening fell like a curtain upon the life of earth, when, weary of speech and busy action, He needed rest for His soul as well as for His body, He would leave His disciples beneath the shelter of some rock or tree and, going up into a mountain nearby, there on the crest of a hill as though on the very edge of the world, He would enfold Himself in the eternal silence.

For Jesus, night was a deliverance and a call. He left the paths of men for God, before whom nature lays down its burden. When night comes the world expands; the earth melts into darkness and leaves us alone with Heaven. We are caught up into the boundless spaces and their torches guide our path. All things bid us mount up higher and open our hearts, and contemplation becomes almost a need. For Christ, in whom contemplation is continuous, it now becomes sweeter and more intense. It is more peaceful, too, and He gladly lingers there.

It may be that sometimes the morning star as it rises finds Him still at prayer. Then the symbol meets the reality; under the rosy wing of morning the star that heralds the day joins its light with Him who called Himself the "Light of the World."[409]

Jesus looks out upon the vibrant ether. I imagine Him intoning a grand hymn in the name of all, giving life and meaning to the stillness, while the adoring silence is enhanced by the fitful cries of the jackal and the owl.

How often He must have sung the words of the Psalm, *Laudate Dominum de coelis:*

> Praise ye the Lord from the heavens:
> praise ye Him in the highest places.

---

[409]John 8:12.

Praise ye Him, all His angels:
>   praise ye Him, all His hosts.

Praise ye Him, O sun and moon:
>   praise Him all ye stars and light.

Praise Him, ye heavens of heavens:
>   and let all the waters above the heavens
>   praise the name of the Lord. . . .

For His name alone is exalted.

Praise of Him is above Heaven and earth.[410]

Jesus is the conductor of this immense choir. Jesus is the leader of praise in creation, and all praises are borne by Him as a light weight is borne upon a wing. From His mountain of prayer He radiates throughout the universe as from a center of life. To all things He gives a soul. He is the living prayer of all beings. His universal mandate constitutes Him as "that which is" confronting "Him who is," and the stars and the spirits look to Him.

His petition follows His adoration. For all, He begs the bread that each needs for his own life: health for our bodies, truth for our minds, love for our hearts, freedom for our wills, fellowship for men; and for all He begs the achievement which is the perfection of beings, and the fruit of that achievement, which is joy.

Jesus asks, and He knows that He receives to the full capacity of those for whom He prays. Nothing can set a limit to His beseeching power, as nothing can limit His power of action, save

[410]Ps. 148:1-4, 13-14 (RSV = Ps. 148:1-5, 13).

the deficiencies of the finite subject who withdraws himself from Him by evil.

Nevertheless, even the imperfection of man's power to receive does not diminish the generosity with which God gives. God always gives all. He has put all things in the hands of Christ, and just as Christ by giving Himself compensates for those men who withhold their gift, so He accepts and utilizes what men cannot receive. His grace is in a manner infinite, as theologians say. It is the fountain from which the grace of all men flows; it is the reservoir into which God pours without need to restrain His munificence.

How is it that the Cross can lend itself to this reciprocal movement and accentuate it with miraculous power? At no time has Jesus prayed more, and at no time has He been better heard. Never on earth has He been in closer communion with the King of Heaven.

Two words, if we rightly understood them, would provide the key to the mystery. The first of these words is *love*, and the second is *sacrifice*.

Love gives value to our worship and efficacy to our prayer. Between persons who are of equal condition, he who loves the more gives the greater honor and receives the greater gifts. The love of Christ for His Father is the soul of His worship, and nowhere does He prove that love better than in the sacrifice of His life: "Greater love than this no man hath, that a man lay down his life for his friends."[411]

The Cross, then, is the great place of prayer, just as it is the great altar, the great monstrance, and the first tabernacle. It is not in vain that we are told to begin and end our prayers with the sign

[411] John 15:13.

224

of the Cross. Properly understood this sign means: "I adore Thee, my God, by the Cross, by Jesus on the Cross, with Jesus on the Cross, as Jesus adored Thee on the Cross, in a spirit of commemoration and trust, but also in a spirit of obedience and sacrifice. . . . I ask of Thee all that I need in the name of the Cross, that is, in the name of the same memory, in the name of the same merits, to which I humbly unite those things that are wanting, according to the exhortation of the Apostle."[412]

∞

The silence of Jesus during His nights of communion with His Father was a completion of the explicit prayers which He had formulated for Himself and for us. On the mountain He gave Himself to ecstasy rather than to words. He remained long absorbed in contemplation, His sacred life plunged deep in the Source of life itself, His arteries throbbing, His heart beating, His mind overwhelmed, His will surrendered, His whole being prostrate in mute and perfect homage.

Have we not said that He is a living homage, a living prayer? His very person is an act of worship. To beseech and to adore He need only say, "Behold me!" Like John the Baptist, and more so than John the Baptist, He is wholly and entirely a *Voice*. When He is not speaking, He is and He loves, and that alone saves us, that alone glorifies the Father of whom no words can rightly speak.

On the Cross these reasons have an added force, and the silence which links the seven Words together is an eloquent commentary upon those mysterious words themselves. The glance upraised to Heaven speaks for itself, and what explanation can add

[412]Col. 1:24.

225

to the tragic significance of that look? Silence, which is the flower of adoration, silence, than which there can be no more eloquent worship when it shelters a desire inspired by love, silence is the equivalent on Calvary of all the prayers which the Master has offered during His life. It contains them all, and with them ours as well. It concentrates them all, and it is from this treasure that the Church will draw when She spreads prayer and praise throughout the world, making them resound like the voice of mighty waters.

∞

Christ looks at Heaven. May we not say now that for the contemplation of Heaven He has no need to open His eyes? Nor need the eyes of His mind turn to any object distinct from Himself; for Christ bears His Heaven within Him.

We cannot here expound the amazing psychology which is involved in the hypostatic union[413] and its consequences. To explain the Heaven that is in Jesus would be to explain the whole doctrine of the Incarnation. But we must take it into account unless we wish to mutilate our theme.

Christ is God and man. Close to us though He shows Himself to be, He is yet "that blessed portion of humanity which God has taken to unite to His divinity," as St. Francis de Sales has said. Of this wondrous union we can have no exact conception; but, happily for the work of our salvation, our minds are not the measure of being.

Our Christ is a living mystery. He bears a name which is incommunicable, "which no man knoweth but Himself."[414] His

---

[413] Namely, the union of divine and human natures in the one person (in Greek, the *hypostasis*) of Jesus Christ.

[414] Rev. 19:12.

name is revealed to Him in a complete intuition, in an intimate contact which none has shared, and this name is the "Word of God,"[415] as well as the "Son of Man."[416] He is "King of Kings and Lord of Lords,"[417] and yet this is still the name of one who is a mortal man.

It follows that Jesus is never fully expressed by anything that He does, says, or thinks on man's plane. It follows that the destiny of man is not the whole of Jesus' destiny considered as a person, nor is His human mission His all. The touch of the God whom He bears within Him, of the God who is Himself, gives Him a higher life. As well as being the envoy and the sublime wayfarer, He is also the traveller who is at home, who no longer needs to arrive.

Humanity is only His workshop, the earth His fulcrum. Precisely because He is given to the world, He communicates with the world only through a narrow gate, that by which God passes to come to men, and through which men come to God.

The rest is all mystery, seclusion, transcendence. Ecstasy is His normal state. He is perpetually enraptured by the consciousness of His divine Sonship, and by the constant irruption of the Divinity, with whom He is one, into all the powers of His being. Ecstasy, which for the mystic is a projection outside the self, for Him is to be in tranquil possession of Himself. Constantly He takes refuge there, where the weight of humanity no longer oppresses. His visible existence is like the flight of a star that has risen from the realms of shadow and is plunging back again. For great hearts, the divine reward is their very greatness. The greatness of all hearts has its sufficiency in itself; in itself it has its incomprehensible source, whence all gifts flow for Him and for all.

[415] Rev. 19:13.
[416] Rev. 1:13.
[417] Rev. 19:16.

In His speech He can do no more than touch upon the unspeakable; but the background which is hidden gives to what He reveals a penetrating force and a creative energy. He unveils mysteries with the opening of His hand. He speaks "as one having authority, and not as the scribes and Pharisees."[418] He is illumined by His own light and passes through our night as though crowned with a halo. He sees clearly and unceasingly that which we perceive only with the intermittent insight of faith. Seeing this, He can express it with certainty. Being master of this, He can inculcate it with the omnipotence of that first Word which creates what It says.

It is from His inner Heaven that Jesus derived the light of the world; it is from the depths of His heart that He sent us His Spirit.

And nature no less than humanity is subject to His life-giving influence. He is the Head of nature as man, while as God He is its Creator and its Providence. Not only the light of souls but also the light of worlds is nourished by Him. In Him the stars have their being and from His life all life issues as a flood. The play of nature stirs the admiration of His human thought and imagination; but the divinity within Him creates it. He is the Wisdom that "plays at all times" before the Principle of all things.[419] He is at once subject to created powers and is Himself the eternal Power that made them.

∞

May we not say that there is within us, in some measure, an imitation of this dualism, of this divinity and this humanity, of which the one is brightness and the other its passing? We, too,

[418] Matt. 7:29.
[419] Prov. 8:30.

have torches within our hearts. Grace, even the depths of nature itself, that something in us which is almost not ourselves, that borders upon the Source of being — what is this if not a sort of human divinity, a participation in that Word which once was given us? While God radiates His light to us by Revelation and through nature, He rises up at the same time from our very depths. On that level where our best thoughts are born, where our graces manifest themselves, God meets Himself. And it is an inner Heaven that we are thus given, a Heaven starred with truths and swept by streams of goodness, a Heaven that is radiant in spite of our night.

∞

It becomes apparent, therefore, that the silence of Jesus, of which we have said that it is more natural to Him than prayer itself, is allied with a solitude untroubled by any human contacts or relations. This same soul which gushes with thoughts and floods with words so that "if they were written every one, the world itself would not be able to contain the books that should be written,"[420] remains at its core an abyss of silence. This soul which is linked with every soul and with every reality, visible and invisible, is in a manner always alone.

In the midst of our busy life Jesus is as detached as He is on His mountain at evening time. The earth counts away its days and nights. Christ counts away His life with the same patient and firm regularity, yet deep within Him is a marvelous repose. He acts, and His mind governs His action. His heart consents, yet He is free. He can ever receive secret messages; He listens to a divine music.

[420]John 21:25.

He fully exemplifies the words of His Apostle: "Our conversation is in Heaven."[421]

∞

Deep beyond all sounding, girt around with solitude and silence, ever seeing and possessing its supreme Object, the soul of Jesus is for this very reason an abyss of happiness. Joy floods that soul and never leaves it; it abides in everlasting day. Pain comes and seizes on that soul. It takes incomparable hold of a sensibility as exquisite as the soul whose sensibility it is. Yet beyond that zone of suffering are wide regions where joy reigns alone.

In Christ there are two lives, the one a temporal life, which moves on from the manger to the Cross and the grave, the other eternal, immutable at the right hand of the Father. The Beatific Vision, identical in each, welds as it were these two lives in one. For Jesus, life after death is not entirely a renewal; it is a continuation. Jesus is reborn and glorified in His flesh; but in His soul He merely pursues His destiny and continues His eternal colloquy with God. The crown of His destiny makes no deep change in Him. In the dust of daily action, and under the searing fire of pain, He was already in glory; He saw God face-to-face. What was there still for Him to acquire, save that His body should finally share the glory of His soul?

Here on earth He is divided. He is an ocean of silence and peace over which roars a tumultuous tide. The tempest assails Him in His Passion, and at the end the "sorrows of death will compass Him."[422] But between these contrary aspects of His life a harmony is heralded, and this harmony is effected in His Ascension.

[421] Phil. 3:20.
[422] Cf. Ps. 114:3 (RSV = Ps. 116:3).

Is it possible thus to associate two states that are opposed the one to the other, each tending to absorb the whole of the soul's vital action: a suffering that is all but permanent with a permanent beatitude, heavenly joy with the Cross? We must associate them. The hypostatic union implies the Beatific Vision as a right; suffering is the appointed means of redemption. It is for the Almighty to reconcile the two. Since the Creator is here united with His handiwork, we cannot suppose that He will recoil from His task, and show Himself incapable of resolving the psychological problem which He Himself has set.

∞

But this is not all. Where so many mysteries already confound us, our theologians seek one mystery more. They seize upon this cry, "My God, my God, why hast Thou forsaken me?"[423] and, without seeing in it (as some do) a cry of despair, they yet lend it a character so poignant that, in comparison with the state of soul it expresses, the agony of the previous day would be little more than nothing. They see in it the very extreme of human anguish.

This interpretation, it must be acknowledged, is not necessitated by the facts. The utterance of Jesus is a quotation from the twenty-first Psalm, of which it forms the opening words. It may therefore quite naturally suggest the idea of a prayer mentally continued, and not of a tragic cry.

The Psalm is prophetic, and it contains the most striking references to the Passion. At the end of it comes a vision of glory with the hope of rich fruits as a result of these sorrows. There is no reason that constrains us to isolate the initial appeal, or to make

---

[423] Ps. 21:1 (RSV = Ps. 22:1).

it anything else but an intonation, or, if it is preferred, a synopsis of the Psalm.

But our theologians have found this simple explanation too superficial; some of them, at least, suspect that there is something beyond. Christ, they think, finds still another dreg at the bottom of His chalice. He has experienced all the torments that man can inflict and now He must suffer one at the hands of God.

The feeling of hope sustains Him: He must lose it. His Father is His one resource against the cruelty and desertion of men; His Father will stand aloof. When earth had cast Him off, He still had His Heaven: this Heaven will now be veiled from His inner gaze, as the sky will be covered with darkness. He must know the taste of Hell!

He will know it under both its forms. The eternal damnation from which He delivers us comprises two pains: the pain of loss and the pain of sense. The first will be represented by His Father's desertion of Him; the second by the Cross. Then only may we say that the Passion is completed, that redemption is accomplished. The tide of sorrow will then have reached its height, and thenceforth can only subside. Otherwise, there would remain one stronghold in the soul of Jesus which had not been attacked.

So be it! Let us rend our hearts, if we will, by the thought that our Savior lost His Heaven in order to win Heaven for us. Let us suppose that He loses it while keeping it still, in the sense that He no longer has experience of it; that He stands before His Father as before an inexorable God — or worse still, that His Father does not appear at all, so that while still in Paradise because He is the Son of God, He yet suffers all the torment of Hell.

"He seems now not to know that He is God," wrote St. Anselm. Some dreadful barrier has arisen between His humanity and His divinity. He feels a sort of malediction upon Him: it is ours, which He has taken upon Himself together with the load of our sins. His bitterness is then indeed infinite, infinite as the love that hides itself away, infinite as the good which He seems to have lost, infinite as the happiness which is gone.

But He loves, and this alleviates the horror of His pain. To the sovereign Good that eludes His grasp He remains attached with such ardent love that His heart cannot be filled with darkness. Can there be despair in One who wills with all His will the will of Him whom He loves? If St. Thérèse was right when she defined Hell as a place in which there is no love, then a Hell in which there is love is already a Heaven. But this Heaven encompassed with darkness is nonetheless for Jesus the extremity of sorrow. His spiritual sun is dead. He is a land without light, bound in ice from pole to pole. Between Himself and His Father the stream of consolation has ceased to flow. His heart's heart has gone out of Him. Think of the pain of the Son of God if He feels that for Him God is no more!

∞

"My God, my God, why hast Thou forsaken me?" This apparent and temporary dereliction has its place, on Calvary, between two phases of confidence and peace — as the agony in the garden was intermediate between the outpourings of the supper room and the sublime courage of the arrest, as a fall comes between two steps. After that trial Jesus regains His tranquillity. His Heaven opens once more; the arms of the Father are once more stretched out to Him. Like St. Stephen later, Jesus sees the heavens opened, and He enters Heaven with the eyes of His soul.

There is another Heaven, and this the last of which we shall take account: the Heaven which He has earned this time, instead of merely contemplating or possessing it; a Heaven which is not only His, but ours. This is His vision of victory, symbolized on

Calvary by those eyes that look out upon the infinity of space through a film of blood.

∽

Is not the sky for us a symbol of this Heaven: a spiritual state remote and sublime in comparison with our present condition, an abode of freedom and peace, a place of delights? Christ has promised us this Heaven, for He said to His disciples at the Last Supper, "I go to prepare a place for you."[424] He has in mind the Ascension, which will appear to situate this mysterious seat of His glory above the clouds. Meanwhile He merits our entry into it.

He who has been constituted an intermediary between God and humanity will surely be able to unite them; He who bears Heaven in Himself will surely be able to open it to us. He is even now knocking at its doors. In a moment He will force them open. Is not this what He says to the good thief: "This day thou shalt be with me in Paradise"?[425]

When early dawn on the Mount of Olives is veiled by a thin layer of mist and the morning star glimmers feebly behind it, it takes little for the rising orb to free itself and soar over the darkness that remains. He, Christ, is this "Morning star that knows no setting, the light that rises from the earth shining serenely in the eyes of mankind."[426]

And now the Heaven to which the living Sun will ascend, and to which all the constellations of human souls are to follow Him, is displayed before His eyes. Jesus looks deep at it with the eyes of the spirit. Without withdrawing His mind from the work at hand,

[424] John 14:2.
[425] Luke 23:43.
[426] *Blessing of the Paschal Candle.*

of which this great future is the object and purpose, He inspects His city, the "city of the air"; the city "crowned with angels as the spouse is crowned by her tresses"[427]; the city of harps and cups of gold, of trumpets and censers, of white robes and palms, of canticles and crowns. It is the city where "God shall wipe all tears from their eyes: and death shall be no more, neither mourning, nor crying, nor sorrow shall be any more, for the former things are passed away."[428]

Jesus looks and His look seems to say, "There lies our way, ye men; I go first and you all follow in my train. The crown is certain. To him that shall overcome, I will give to sit with me on my throne: as I also have overcome, and am set down with my Father on His throne.[429] Be ye all with me for the great victory, and since there is no victory without suffering, let us suffer. Since victory presupposes a holy death, let us die, and, prepare with me for a holy death. Blessed, now, are the dead who die in the Lord."

"From henceforth now," answers the Spirit, "they may repose from their labors; for their works follow them."[430]

---

[427] "Hymn for the Dedication of a Church."
[428] Rev. 21:4.
[429] Rev. 3:21.
[430] Rev. 14:13.

Epilogue

The end draws slowly on. Jesus takes His last draught of gall, which reminds Him of all the others that He has taken. His increasing pain makes Him feel that the last flame of life is leaping up in Him. His work is finished; the tree has now only to grow. He has accomplished His task. Its consequences in the course of ages need Christ no longer; indeed, they would exclude His presence: "It is expedient to you," He said, "that I go."[431]

The Scriptures are fulfilled in Him; all that He had to do is done, and He has suffered all that He had to suffer. He assembles all these things in His mind, and expresses them in one utterance, as though signifying to Death that it may now approach its Master:

"It is consummated."

All is indeed consummated for Him, and therefore also for us. Man can ask nothing more, and Jesus, who had resolved to give

---

[431] John 16:7.

beyond all for which man could ask, has nothing more to give. He has restored all things in Himself, and His Cross will remain forever lifted up between Heaven and earth, bringing all blessings to earth and warding off all evil. What more had He desired, and what more could He accomplish?

∞

The final portents appear as the ninth hour approaches. The night of Golgotha thickens; Gareb is draped as a catafalque. The blackness heralds the great light which is to come.

The earth trembles; a strange commotion takes place among the tombs, and dead men come forth. The veil of the Temple — perhaps carried away by a violent wind, the black sirocco which is supposed to bring darkness in its train — is torn from top to bottom. This is the first veil, that which separates the vestibule from the Holy Place. It reveals the secrets of Christ and the mysteries which Christ has taught, leaving only, behind the veil of the Holy of Holies, the greatest mystery of all.

Such is God's demonstration. If He uses nature in making it, this is only one more example of the harmony of His works. He proclaims His terrible mercy in the language of events.

Jerusalem huddles its pale domes under the cloud as the hen of the parable gathers her chickens. There lies the city of blood, already a corpse, under the Roman's lifted sword.

There is no brightness in nature; there is no brightness in the closed hearts of men. Only the love of the saintly group rises up to the suffering Savior; only the love of Jesus covers the world.

Magdalene is still sobbing; a little further away the holy women are watching. The few disciples are silent; John is supporting his "mother," who is broken but unbending, erect though ready to succumb. If the very stones are rent, what of her heart!

Jesus is exhausted and allows His final strength to ebb slowly away. He gasps for breath and a burning thirst still devours Him. But the fever of that thirst is chiefly spiritual; He thirsts for the earth, and the earth, without knowing it, thirsts for Him. Would He not wish to give one more kiss with those poor twisted lips to this earth that He loves? Would He not even in His lowliness once more, for today and for all time, offer His cheek to the traitor's kiss?

His bloodless body is ready for the tomb; His soul is ready for its God.

Before His eyes the landscape begins now to fade away. Moab has long since vanished in the darkness; the outlines of the Mount of Olives and the slopes of Zion become dimmed into space. The Cenacle and the palace of Herod, the Temple and the Antonia, the walls with the yawning Gate of Ephraim, the very hill of Golgotha itself — all becomes dark. The anemones have dulled their crimson hue; the crimson drops on His brow harden beneath the cruel crown.

Yet Jesus is in full possession of Himself. "No man taketh His life from Him"; He will "lay it down" Himself.[432] He will lay it down in the hands of His Father:

"Father, into Thy hands I commend my spirit."[433]

All things are in the hand of God; but that hand wills to receive all things from the freedom which He makes the associate of His power. The freedom of Christ renders Him this sovereign homage. His last gesture is like His first: "Behold I come."[434] This is the keynote and the consummation of His whole life. It is a gesture of trust and love, of union and of surrender. All men must

[432] John 10:17-18.
[433] Luke 23:46.
[434] Rev. 3:11, 22:7, 12.

share it because it is made on their behalf, and the elect of all ages
and of all worlds will reap its fruit.

∞

And now, having nothing further on this earth to do, ready to
surrender His life, to lay His head on His breast so that its crown
forms a halo about His heart, having nothing more to contemplate
with this glance which now meets the supreme Mystery of all,

Jesus closes His eyes.

Biographical Note

Antonin Gilbert Sertillanges

(1863-1948)

Born in the French city of Clermont-Ferrand on November 16, 1863, A. G. Sertillanges entered the Dominican order twenty years later, taking the religious name Dalmatius. In 1888 he was ordained a priest.

After completing his studies and teaching for a few years, Fr. Sertillanges was appointed secretary of the prestigious scholarly journal *Revue Thomiste*. In 1900 he became professor of moral theology at the Catholic Institute in Paris, where he taught for twenty years. Later, Fr. Sertillanges taught elsewhere in France and also in Holland. During his year-long stay in Jerusalem in 1923, he was inspired to write *What Jesus Saw from the Cross*.

His classic book *The Intellectual Life* explains the methods, conditions, habits, and virtues that are necessary in the intellectual life. These virtues bore great fruit in Fr. Sertillanges' own life, enabling him to become a widely recognized expert in the philosophy of St. Thomas Aquinas and to write many books and over a thousand articles in the areas of philosophy, theology, art, and spirituality.

But Fr. Sertillanges was far more than a professor and scholar. During his lifetime, he was widely admired for his skill as a preacher, a spiritual director, and an apologist, and was particularly successful in presenting the Faith in compelling terms to the young and to the unconverted.

No "ivory tower" intellectual, but first and foremost a passionate son of the Church, Fr. Sertillanges' numerous works bridge the gap that often yawns today between academic theology and the everyday faith of the ordinary layman.

The fruit of both hard study and devout prayer, and motivated by the desire to preach Catholic truth *usque ad mortem* ("unto death," in the words of the Dominican motto), the works of Fr. Sertillanges are now informing and inspiring yet another generation of readers in these times of theological uncertainty and moral disarray.

An Invitation

Reader, the book that you hold in your hands was published by Sophia Institute Press.

Sophia Institute seeks to restore man's knowledge of eternal truth, including man's knowledge of his own nature, his relation to other persons, and his relation to God.

Our press fulfills this mission by offering translations, reprints, and new publications. We offer scholarly as well as popular publications; there are works of fiction along with books that draw from all the arts and sciences of our civilization. These books afford readers a rich source of the enduring wisdom of mankind.

Sophia Institute Press is the publishing arm of the Thomas More College of Liberal Arts and Holy Spirit College. Both colleges are dedicated to providing university-level education in the Western tradition under the guiding light of Catholic teaching.

If you know a young person who might be interested in the ideas found in this book, share it. If you know a young person seeking a college that takes seriously the adventure of learning and the quest for truth, bring our institutions to his attention.

www.SophiaInstitute.com
www.ThomasMoreCollege.edu
www.HolySpiritCollege.org

SOPHIA INSTITUTE PRESS

THE PUBLISHING DIVISION OF

Sophia Institute Press® is a registered trademark of Sophia Institute. Sophia Institute is a tax-exempt institution as defined by the Internal Revenue Code, Section 501(c)(3). Tax I.D. 22-2548708.